Commit!

COMMIT!

*Make Your Mind and Body Stronger
and Unlock Your Full Potential*

ENDA MCNULTY

PENGUIN BOOKS

To my mother and father, who have been amazing in their love, support, inspiration and empowerment – thank you for allowing me to live my dreams.

And to Julia, who has given me all the love, support and commitment in the world – thank you for your love and for inspiring me to be better in everything I do.

PENGUIN BOOKS

UK | USA | Canada | Ireland | Australia
India | New Zealand | South Africa

Penguin Books is part of the Penguin Random House group of companies
whose addresses can be found at global.penguinrandomhouse.com.

Penguin
Random House
UK

First published by Penguin Ireland 2017
Published in Penguin Books 2018

001

Copyright © Enda McNulty, 2017

The moral right of the author has been asserted

Printed in Great Britain by Clays Ltd, St Ives plc

A CIP catalogue record for this book is available from the British Library

ISBN: 978–0–241–97884–9

www.greenpenguin.co.uk

MIX
Paper from
responsible sources
FSC
www.fsc.org
FSC® C018179

Penguin Random House is committed to a
sustainable future for our business, our readers
and our planet. This book is made from Forest
Stewardship Council® certified paper.

CONTENTS

Preface   1

MINDSET

1 The open mind   11
2 Changing your mindset   23
3 Building a growth mindset   32
   Mindset – take action now!   47

MISSION

4 Meaning   51
5 Name it   66
6 Staying the distance   79
   Mission – take action now!   92

ENERGY

7 Get moving   95
8 Eating, sleeping and staying on track   112
   Energy – take action now!   127

RESILIENCE

9   Bouncing back   131
10   Resilience in action   149
    Resilience – take action now!   157

MENTAL STRENGTH

11   Comfortable in the Coliseum   161
12   Getting tough   171
13   Think your way into better performance   183
14   The power of visualization   193
    Mental strength – take action now!   203

FLOW

15   Getting in the zone   207
16   When dreams come true   220

Reading list   229
Acknowledgements   231

PREFACE

Jim McCartan was in charge of running the football squads at the Abbey Grammar in Newry, where I went to school. He was a small but powerfully built man with piercing blue eyes and Paul Newman looks. You never saw him out of his tracksuit, no matter what he was teaching, and he spoke in a deep voice that came from somewhere down around his boots. A hugely talented footballer in his day, he commanded great respect at the school.

I was fourteen years old, and had missed the first three training sessions of the year. Jim came looking for me during class the Monday after the third missed session.

'I see you haven't been at training, Enda, what's going on?'

'Sorry, sir,' I shrugged, 'I wasn't feeling great.'

'Will you be there tomorrow?'

'I'll be there, yes, sir.'

'OK, see you in the PE room at half three.'

I didn't show.

The next day, I met him in the hall. He fixed me with those penetrating blue eyes and asked what had happened.

'Ah, sir, I'm still not feeling great, sir.'

'I'll tell you what, Enda,' he said, 'I'll see you on Saturday morning at half ten. That gives you three days. Will you be ready to go on Saturday morning?'

I told him I would, but again I didn't show up.

The following week, I was in geography class when there was a knock at the door. I looked up and saw his face through the glass.

'Excuse me, Mr Mooney, could I speak to Enda McNulty for a second, please?'

I came out into the hall and he closed the door after me.

'Enda, why were you not at training on Saturday morning?'

'Ah, sir, to be honest with you, I was still feeling –'

Before I could tell him what I was feeling, I felt his hand on my chest and he pushed me back against the wall. I blinked and Jim's face was inches from my own. He didn't say anything for a second but stared hard at me.

'Enda,' he said eventually, 'do you realize what the biggest waste in life is? Do you?'

'No, sir.'

'The biggest waste in life is waste of potential. You have potential and you're wasting it. Don't grow up and don't grow old with potential you never used. If you don't invest in it, you lose it.'

He tightened his grip. 'I'll give you one more chance, Enda. Training's on Tuesday after school. If you're not there, I'm giving up on you.'

He let go and walked away, while I stood there, staring at his retreating back.

I was there on the Tuesday and I never missed a training session by choice for the rest of my life.

Wake-up calls. I've had a lot of them in my career. I'll be eternally grateful to Jim McCartan for one of the first.

*

This book is about everything that followed from that first wake-up call.

It's about everything I've been taught by the people who mentored me and gave me the tools to help myself.

It's about the lessons learned from fifteen years of working with kids, with parents, with elite sports people, CEOs and all kinds of organizations, helping them to realize their potential.

The decision to commit lies at the heart of this work. You can think of the idea of commitment as a tired old cliché, but the truth is that unless you commit to something, you're going nowhere. Unless you decide that this is what you must do, and then lock on to that something, you're stuck in neutral.

THE TRUTH IS THAT UNLESS YOU COMMIT TO SOMETHING, YOU'RE GOING NOWHERE.

This book explores the idea of committing from all angles.

In the first section, I look at the change in mindset needed to bring about genuine lasting change, exploring the ways in which you can reinvent your psychology to deliver on your potential.

The second section is all about creating a plan for change, and how to stick to that plan when the going gets tough.

Energy management is a central part of my philosophy. In the third section of the book, I look at the commitment you need to make to exercise, nutrition, rest and recovery in order to deliver the energy to live fully.

Resilience – the ability to bounce back from adversity – is the central subject of the fourth section.

Mental strength goes hand in hand with resilience. In the fifth section, I explore a range of techniques to boost your mental toughness, drawing on the inspiration of a range of elite, and not-so-elite, athletes and performers.

Finally, I look at the concepts of flow and living in the now – which is the only place we can live.

It's amazing how many of us are going through the motions every day, how many of us have vague notions of what we might like to do next year or the year after, but who find ourselves looking back with regret at all the things we never did.

It's a kind of paralysis. We're all fearful and anxious, plagued by doubt. Every one of us has an internal critic.

Imagine you committed to breathing life into your dreams every single day. What if you were to just step up and do it?

Don't just dip a toe in the water. Dive in. Immerse yourself.

Don't be fooled when you look at elite performers – on the stage, on the pitch, in the boardroom – doing things you couldn't ever dream of doing. They may seem invincible, unbeatable, so in command of themselves that they scarcely appear human. But the truth is that at one point or another everyone suffers from low self-confidence.

Doubt and fear are universal.

When Armagh played Dublin in the 2002 All-Ireland semi-final, this was the biggest game of football that Armagh had been involved in since the All-Ireland final of 1977, which we lost. I was sick with nerves. We ran out on to the pitch and got hit by a wall of sound. It was dizzying. I felt like a lost little lamb. The stadium was packed to the rafters, it was rattling. Walking in the parade behind the band, my legs were shaking – I wasn't sure I was going to make it round the pitch. I started to think about ways out of it. I thought about going up to Joe Kernan, the manager. He knew that I was having trouble with my hamstrings. I decided I would go up to him and pretend I'd pulled a hamstring. I decided to tell him that I couldn't play.

But I did play – and I had arguably the best game of my career.

How?

Because of everything I had done up to that point, because of the preparations I had been laying since I was fourteen years old. Because the work I had done over the previous ten years had been all about this moment.

A week before he went out to defend his European Indoor 400m championship gold medal in Birmingham, Irish Olympian David Gillick was also wrestling with doubt. He was the defending champion and had moved to England to work more intensively on his training. He felt a weight of expectation.

What if he ran flat?

Wouldn't everyone think he had made a big mistake moving?

What if he lost his funding?

What if he embarrassed himself?

A week later, David retained his European title and won gold for a second time.

Why?

Because he had committed to himself. He had prepared. He had put together a plan, a complete plan that left no stone unturned in his quest for what he knew he could achieve. He found a way to deal with the doubt that plagues every one of us – and a way to win despite it.

*

The other thing you may tell yourself about people who are great at what they do is that they're simply very talented. That it's lucky for them to be so naturally gifted. But talent is over-rated. When Armagh won the All-Ireland in 2002, there were better footballers sitting at home on their couches in Armagh, watching that match. There were better Armagh footballers in the stands, looking down at us on the pitch. What defined that team was not talent, but character.

I wasn't the best footballer, not by a long stretch. A guy called John Toal, who played midfield, wasn't the most talented footballer, but he was a dog of war. There was a guy called Kieran Hughes at wing halfback. He never started a match in the All-Ireland winning year, but he had played in 1998, 1999, 2000. He laid tar for a living. If you've a battle before you, you want a guy who lays tar for a living at wing halfback. Francie Bellew – you couldn't say he was the most talented guy in the world, but he would go for a ball he probably shouldn't go for, and win it.

WE ALL HAVE STRENGTHS, WE CAN ALL PLAN, WE CAN ALL WORK HARD, WE CAN ALL BUILD CHARACTER.

The point is that you do not need inbuilt – 'Sure, he was born with it' – talent. You don't have to be gifted. We all have strengths, we can all plan, we can all work hard, we can all build character.

Character is a decision.

Part of building character is understanding and working on the obstacles you put in your own way.

You may have these mental blocks. You may be haunted by thoughts of missed opportunities, voices in your head whispering that it's too late:

'I wish I had an MBA.'

'I wish I'd looked after myself better in my twenties.'

'I wish I had studied in college.'

'I wish I hadn't thrown away that relationship.'

Or you may be facing practical challenges – the loss of a job, illness in the family, a business falling apart.

A lot of people don't want to know what's holding them back. They blame their situation on their mother, their father, their upbringing, their school, their current or previous boss, their partner, their coach, the government, the economy . . .

They don't really want to face the reality, which is this: *the biggest thing holding you back is you.*

It's all down to you.

Whatever is holding you back, the truth is that you have the resources to deal with it. What you need, you've already got inside. It's a matter of harnessing your inner strengths to get where you want to go.

If you were forced to take meaningful action to unleash your potential, where would you start?

If you had ninety days to transform your life, what would you do?

If you had ninety days to put right all the wrongs and to do only things that are important, meaningful and fulfilling – things that would be memorable for the rest of your life – what would that be like?

This book is all about those next ninety days.

So, commit. Take the course, quit the job, go to the audition, haul yourself kicking and screaming out of your comfort zone.

Not next year, not next week.

Take action now, and tomorrow, and the next day, to become your best self.

MINDSET

1

THE OPEN MIND

I run a company called McNulty Performance. Our vision is to be a game-changing company that transforms human potential globally. Our mission is to inspire people to be at their best every day. For the last ten years, we've been working with all kinds of people from all walks of life, helping them to realize their potential and perform to the best of their abilities. It's work that has taken us all over the world.

But before all that, I worked as a professional sports coach and as a performance psychologist.

About twelve or thirteen years ago, I was asked to do a session with a rugby team at St Mary's College in Rathmines. They were struggling and in danger of being relegated. I was in the dressing room to give a talk about mental preparation before one of their regular training sessions. It was March and still bitterly cold. The dressing room was small, box-like and very basic. There was no heating, and the squad was sitting huddled in there, blowing into their hands, looking forward to getting out on the pitch and getting warmed up.

It didn't help that it was so cold, but almost everyone in that room did not want me to be there. 'Sports psychologist?'

I could hear muttering and sniggering. Most were half turned from me, chatting amongst themselves, their body language indicating that they'd like me to stop speaking and get out of their dressing room as quickly as possible.

But there was one guy – tall, slender, black hair – who was sitting alone and alert on the bench, utterly focused on what I was saying, despite the fact that he knew nothing about me. Throughout that forty-minute session, his concentration never flagged. He was completely engaged. Though he never spoke, his focus – his unwavering fix upon what I was saying – was like an independent force in the room.

Afterwards I asked the coach, 'Who's that young fella, the tall one, dark hair.'

'His name is Jonathan Sexton.'

I never forgot that single-minded focus, that openness to learning something new. Now, every time I see it, I remember that bleak March afternoon and Johnny Sexton's hunger to learn.

Ten years later, I was working with a sales team in Dublin. We were doing a session called 'Step Up to Your Potential' in the Radisson Hotel in Stillorgan.

The room was full of pharmaceutical reps and sales managers. I had done my homework beforehand and I knew that the company hadn't been doing that well. Sales were sluggish, earnings for the three previous quarters had come in well below forecasts.

You develop an instinct after a while. You look around and you can tell who are the Sextons in the room – who are the people who want to learn, who really want to up their game. And you can tell too which ones are happy enough where they are and just want this to be over so they can go get lunch.

We began with a series of activities designed to get everyone motivated, to get them thinking about ways of boosting their performance in the year ahead. Within five minutes, I had picked out four people in the audience who were as engaged in the session as Johnny Sexton had been that day in St Mary's.

I set the participants the exercise of creating individual master plans, detailing everything they would do to make change happen. We spent the whole day on this process, with the aim of creating living, breathing documents that would provide step-by-step guides for the work that had to be done.

When we completed the exercise, it was those same four people who had put the most work into it. Not only had they filled out their plans in minute detail but their engagement was obvious from the neatness of their handwriting, the care that had gone into everything they had listed. You only had to glance at one of their plans to know that these people were deeply committed to fulfilling their potential. They wanted to up their skills and improve their knowledge. They knew things could be better and they wanted to find a way to make that happen.

This was an eight-hour session but throughout, the energy of these four people – all of whom were sitting in different parts of the room – never wavered. You'd see other people half-heartedly filling in their templates, or texting under the tables, but these people were there, present in the room, fully engaged.

And at the end of the session, who came up looking for advice on what books they should read, on what TED talks they should watch, on where they could find the best coaches?

Those same four.

When we had finished, the Head of Sales made an announcement. 'Just to give you guys an extra incentive, next March the top performers will get an all-expenses, four-night stay in Rome in a five-star hotel, over the weekend of the Ireland–Italy rugby game.'

The following March, I was in Rome for the game. I had begun working with the Irish rugby team and this was the first time I had travelled with them. I was in the famous Harry's Bar on the Via Veneto with a couple of friends who'd come over for the match. It was around half nine when the door bursts open and who dances into the bar?

That's right, the four people who had impressed me at the drug company training session almost a year earlier.

Sure, it was a coincidence that I happened to be in the same place that night, but it was no coincidence that these four people had won themselves that trip. What they had, and have – what Sexton has – is not simply an innate talent. It's an ability to see that improvement is possible, and then to act on that.

They have what's known as a growth mindset.

Born with it?

Mindset is a set of beliefs or a way of thinking that determines our outlook and our attitude, and therefore our actions and behaviour. If we have a *growth* mindset, our beliefs, our attitude, our way of thinking inform the kinds of actions and behaviour that allow us to grow. By contrast, a *fixed* mindset is one in which our attitude, beliefs and way of thinking feed into behaviour that keeps us just as we are.

I am what I am

A fixed mindset locks you into your current life. With a fixed mindset, nothing is ever going to change, not really. Even if the best opportunity in the world comes along, a fixed mindset will prevent you from taking it, because you will think:

'I've never done anything like that before, so I won't be able for it.'

WITH A FIXED MINDSET, NOTHING IS EVER GOING TO CHANGE, NOT REALLY.

'There's far too much risk involved in taking that leap, I can't afford for this to go wrong.'

'This isn't exactly what I was looking for, I think I'll wait for something better.'

Someone with a fixed mindset believes that Johnny Sexton was born with God-given talent that explains his success.

Someone with a fixed mindset believes that she can't get any better at her job.

Someone with a fixed mindset believes that he can't become more intelligent.

Someone with a fixed mindset believes that because her mother was overweight, she is destined to be overweight.

Someone with a fixed mindset believes that he's not supposed to be a great communicator, because some people are just useless at explaining themselves.

Someone with a fixed mindset believes that the glass ceiling will stop her from becoming a leader in her organization.

Someone with a fixed mindset believes that some people are destined for greatness, while others – like them – are destined to remain at a humdrum level for ever.

Someone with a fixed mindset believes: *I am what I am and nothing can change it.*

People with a fixed mindset don't seek new opportunities, they don't seek feedback, they don't look for coaching or mentoring, they're not interested in growth or development. They will never leave their comfort zones.

Why?

Because they don't tend to believe that they can become great doctors, or great teachers or great mothers or great musicians.

The fixed mindset takes a pessimistic view of human potential. It tells you that talent, intelligence and sporting prowess are fixed, immovable qualities that you either have or you don't.

The fixed mindset tells you that effort is pointless, that if you fail, you weren't smart enough or talented enough. And that's the end of the story.

And with a fixed mindset, you don't just fail, you *are* a failure.

Raising the bar

At the other end of the spectrum you have the growth mindset.

Someone with a growth mindset may know that their current job isn't perfect, but they also know that if they work at it, they could transform it into the dream job.

Someone with a growth mindset might not be that fit, but they realize this: 'How fit I am today is irrelevant. If I work at this for the next twelve months, I can be incredibly fit.'

Someone with a growth mindset believes that they can become expert in a new skill. They know that when they fail, it's an opportunity to start again, more intelligently.

Someone with a growth mindset believes that they can improve their emotional intelligence; they are always looking for coaching and feedback and mentoring.

Someone with a growth mindset is reading constantly, engaging with new ideas and approaches.

Someone with a growth mindset is always looking to raise the bar.

Again, this has nothing to do with talent. The first time I met Johnny Sexton, I knew nothing about his ability on the rugby pitch. I only knew that he was hungry to learn and improve. But could he have achieved all he has without that hunger?

The growth mindset is full of possibility. A growth mindset re-defines failure.

THE GROWTH MINDSET IS FULL OF POSSIBILITY.

If you fail, you're not handed a label you have to wear for life; instead, you are given an opportunity to figure stuff out, to learn, to grow.

Mindset can be changed

This is the good news. The reality is that if you change your mindset, your behaviour will follow. Changing your mindset will allow you to take control of your life, rather than letting your life control you.

If you doubt that it's possible to change your outlook, I am pleased to tell you that you're wrong. Time and again over the course of my work with all kinds of people, I've seen hard work, application and character trump talent. That's not to say that talent isn't important – it is. But without application, work and the motivating and enlightening power of failure, it's not much use to anyone.

I have no doubt that the Armagh football team's failures throughout the late nineties and at the beginning of the noughties showed us where we were going wrong, and contributed directly to our ultimate success in 2002.

American psychologist Carol Dweck is the authority in this area. In her groundbreaking book *Mindset*, she explores the difference between a growth mindset and a fixed mindset and shows that the debate over how and why people differ, and whether or not real change is possible, has gone on for ever. Dweck points out that one surprising champion of the view that experiences, training and ways of learning shape intelligence was Alfred Binet, the inventor of the IQ test. We think of IQ as unchangeable, a rigid measure of how smart, or otherwise, you are. The truth, however, is that Binet designed the test to identify children who were not benefiting from the public school system in Paris.

Why?

So that the system could be adapted to help get them back on track.

We're also seeing an increasing body of research which confirms what I've observed with our clients, time and again. People have a much greater capacity for brain development than we think.

PEOPLE HAVE A MUCH GREATER CAPACITY FOR BRAIN DEVELOPMENT THAN WE THINK.

Michael Merzenich is an American neuroscientist who's done pioneering work in the area of brain plasticity. His research has proved that the brain isn't hardwired at all, but can rewire itself continually over the course of your life. He believes that 'brain aerobics' should be part of a well-organized life, in the same way that physical exercise is.

Science is telling us that you are in charge, that it's under your control, that your happiness, your well-being, your abilities, your capacities are capable of continuous modification, continuous improvement, and you're the responsible agent and party.[1]

While I was a student at Queen's University Belfast, I played centre back on the Sigerson Cup team – the Sigerson being the senior inter-varsity Gaelic football competition. The whole experience of Sigerson football was wonderful. I made some great friends and had some formative experiences – none more so than the 2000 final which we played in Galway against University College Dublin (UCD).

The nature of Sigerson is such that you're not going to play in front of big crowds, you're not going to play on lovely pitches, you're not going to get world-class referees. The competition is played out in the depths of winter. It's dogged, it's rugged, it's relentless. And because it's such a test of your character, there's a kind of brotherhood among the guys who have played it. I meet them from time to time, in different places all over the world, and we all share that bond.

The 2000 final was played in late February, and conditions were as bad as Sigerson conditions could be. The pitch in Moycullen, Co. Galway, was barely playable. It had been raining most of the weekend, and it was little better than a bog.

This was our third game in a row. We'd played the quarter-final two days earlier, and the semi-final the day before. It was gruelling stuff, especially after very vigorous club and county campaigns over the previous twelve months. Heavy,

1 From Merzenich's 2004 TED talk, 'Growing Evidence of Brain Plasticity'.

wet winter pitches aren't just more difficult to play on, they also suck the energy out of your legs, leaving you so much more tired than you would be after playing on a good surface.

This story isn't about that, though; this story is about Dessie Ryan. It was in Queen's that I met Dessie for the first time. He was to become one of the biggest influences on my life – both at that time and in the years to come. He was the head coach of the university team. At about five foot seven, he's rugged, athletic and lean. Like Jim McCartan, he always wore a tracksuit and was and remains superfit.[2]

Dessie had put in four years trying to get us to the final of the Sigerson, and we had finally made it. We were playing what was – on paper at least – a much more talented UCD team. They were the city slickers, the best resourced team in the country.

Or at least, that's what we told ourselves. That's what we believed.

I remember on the way down to Galway in the bus, Dessie told us the story of Hernán Cortés, the Spanish conquistador who arrived in Mexico with a small force of 600 Spaniards. He inspired his troops to victory in the campaign that followed by issuing one instruction: 'Burn the boats.' The choice before them then became simple. Win, or die.

---

2 At seventy-four, Dessie Ryan is still one of the fittest men I've ever known. Only last week I phoned him – I try to call him at least once a month – and when he answered, he was panting.

'What's up with you, Dessie?'

'I was doing a bit of skipping.'

'Skipping? For how long?'

'An hour.'

The final wasn't pretty, but then that was Sigerson football. Moycullen was so bad that afternoon, there was water coming up out of the pitch. I was centre half back and I could hardly see the full forward at the other end of the pitch. And as a spectacle it was awful.

We slogged it out, back and forth, for an hour before the whole thing ended in a draw. We went back inside, I dropped down on the bench and looked around me. The changing room, which was tiny, was packed with drenched, exhausted bodies. You could see the steam rising from them. Nobody spoke; there was just panting and muttering.

I could see that we were a spent force. Sodden, covered in mud, shattered. Everyone was bent over, heads down, not looking at each other. We were flogged, we were gone.

At that point there was some confusion over whether there would be extra time or a replay. We did know, however, that the opposition were fresher than us. They'd had an easy run through to the final from the quarter-final, they'd barely had to push themselves. From the dressing room, we could all hear the wind rising, driving the rain in bursts against the window.

It was over.

I knew it, we knew it, everyone knew it.

There was a scuffling sound outside, then the dressing-room door burst open. There stood Dessie, all five foot seven of him, his eyes blazing. I could see the mark in the door where he'd kicked it in.

He flew into the middle of the room.

'These lads don't want to play extra time!' he roared. 'They're not up for it! They don't have the courage to go out there, they don't have the balls for it!'

He spun round, looking every single one of us in the eye.

'Well, if they think we're going for a replay, they've got another thing coming. We're going to play this game now. We're going to play it. Are ye ready for it? Are ye?'

Everyone in that dressing room sprang up. I've never seen anything like it. One minute we were a beaten docket, the next we were ready for anything.

They didn't want to play it. They weren't up for it. They were weak.

We went into a huddle and I started to roar at them.

'We're going to play it now! We're going to play it now, we're going to beat these guys! We're going to do what it takes to win this game!'

We went out.

And we won.

Afterwards we found out that, far from not wanting to play, the UCD team were all on to keep going. Dessie had made it all up. And with that little bit of improvisation, he transformed the mental state of the players. He switched our mindset from fixed – *there is nothing we can do about this* – to growth – *there are possibilities here* – just like that. He didn't wave a wand and turn us into better footballers than the other team, but he changed our beliefs in an instant.

Those new beliefs changed what we thought. And with that came new resolve, and a new way of behaving.

It was genius – one of the greatest feats of psychological deception that I've ever seen. It demonstrated that, with the right tools, beliefs can be reset, behaviours changed and results radically improved.

It proved to me the importance of mindset in any endeavour.

2

CHANGING YOUR MINDSET

Throughout my life I've been lucky in that I've always been surrounded by people who were willing to help me improve, starting with my mum and dad, but also the people I met through football – leaders like Dessie Ryan, and my old team mate Kieran McGeeney.

Look at the most successful people in the world. They never go it alone. The best CEOs always surround themselves with talented people to challenge them, to help them perform to the limits of their ability.

This is why I believe that the best way to help you shift from a fixed to a growth mindset is to get help. Find a coach. An external view is so powerful in helping to identify the changes that need to be made in the first place, and then keeping you focused on the process of moving up and getting better, week after week, month after month.

Working with a coach

The first time I met Padraic Moyles, he had been the lead dancer in *Riverdance* for ten years. He was twenty-seven years old and on top of his game. But he was concerned about the ten years to come. 'I want to be better than myself,' he told me. 'I want to be better than the best.'

What impressed me most about Padraic that first day was his hunger to learn. Despite being among the leading performers in his profession, despite being in peak physical condition, he was still looking for a way to get better, a way to get more out of himself.

'I don't want you telling me I'm good,' he told me that first day, 'I want you to tell me how I'm going to be the best.'

....
'I WANT YOU TO TELL ME HOW I'M GOING TO BE THE BEST.'
....

This was 2007, and Padraic was looking over his shoulder at the guys coming up behind him, who wanted what he had. After ten years at the top, he knew he was vulnerable and that if he became complacent, he would surrender his position to someone else.

Despite the fact that he knew he was in great shape, he had a full physical done. The stress test couldn't put Padraic under stress. His resting heart rate was in the high 30s, low 40s. You only find that kind of heart rate in a handful of supremely fit athletes. The average would be between 60 and 100 beats per minute. He had about 9% or 10% body fat, compared to an average in the general population of between 18% and 24%. These results would reassure most people.

Not Padraic.

'My fear was going downhill. I'd always heard about people reaching their peak between twenty-five and twenty-eight. I was twenty-seven. I began to wonder how long I could stay at that level without letting anyone get ahead of me . . . My big fear was that I would stay too long, that one day some-one would come up to me, put a hand on my shoulder and say, "It's over, it's time for you to move on."'

Padraic laid all of this out the first time we met. While I wasn't sure what I could do for Padraic, I thought that he could probably help me.

At that time I was getting feedback that my delivery wasn't good enough. People would say, 'Enda, you're speaking too fast,' or, 'You're mumbling, we can't make out a word you're saying.' The first time I stood up in front of the Leinster rugby team to talk to them about mental toughness, the non-Irish players hadn't a clue what I was saying.

One of the guys on the Armagh team used to slag me continually. He made out that I sounded just like the guy behind the counter in a well-known local shop at home who was notoriously difficult to understand. He used to take me off, mumbling over his words and growling. It drove me crazy.

My job is all about communication. If people can't under-stand me, what the hell is the point in speaking?

So I got coaching on my communication skills.

I slowed down my delivery, I began to take greater care over how I pronounced words. I spent a lot of time watching great communicators in action, absorbing how they spoke, how they connected with their audience.

I realized that great communication isn't just about mak-ing yourself understood. So much of how we connect with others is non-verbal. It's about performance. That's why I was so eager to work with Padraic.

'You can learn from me,' I told him, 'if I can learn from you.'

Padraic explained that, as far as he was concerned, performance was all about one thing.

> 'I want each person who comes to a show to feel like they're the only person in the audience. When I make eye contact with them, do they feel the energy? Do they feel that I love what I'm doing? Do they feel the passion coming off the stage? Those are the sorts of things I always want as a direct result of my performance.'

Not long after I first met Padraic, I went along to see him in action. His performance blew me away. Not just the energy and the passion. What struck me was the way he connected with the audience. I hadn't told him that I was coming to the show, but I could tell he had spotted me because he looked at me constantly.

Afterwards he told me he had no idea I was there.

I said, 'I need to learn that sort of eye contact. I need to learn how to perform on a stage in front of people the same way you perform on that stage.'

So we started working on my communication skills, and he showed me how to start connecting with people in just the way that he did it.

In the meantime, in my work with him, I brought the rest of the team on board. Our strength and conditioning expert tested his hydration levels. We looked at what he was doing prior to the show – his warm-up, his cool-down, his nutrition. We took it all apart and examined it minutely.

Straight away, we could see that while Padraic was doing a lot of the right things, he was also doing a lot of the wrong things. We encouraged him to make a radical change in how he approached show days.

'If the show was at eight o'clock, I would dance the entire thing, start to finish, at four p.m. The fitness coach said that was like driving to Mayo and back to warm yourself up for driving to Mayo and back. So I stopped all of that, and instead put together a strengthening warm-up that was effective but didn't put quite as much mileage on the clock.'

At the same time, we continued to work on his preparation, his routines, his nutrition, his rest and recovery, his weekly planning, fine-tuning all of it to the point where there was no element that hadn't been tailored to his needs.

This approach is based around the concept of marginal gains popularized by Sir Dave Brailsford, performance director of British Cycling. When he took up that position, he began identifying the individual components of winning races, with the aim of improving each one – if only marginally. He introduced a range of small innovations, for example:

→ He improved the aerodynamic profile of the bike.
→ He improved the mechanics area where the bikes were maintained.
→ He got the team to start using antibacterial hand gel to cut down on infections.
→ He redesigned the team bus to make it more comfortable and to improve the team's rest and recuperation.

Each change delivered a tiny improvement, but added together, these improvements made a very significant difference to performance, making Team GB the best in world cycling.

We applied the same approach to Padraic's lifestyle, training and preparation.

'I believe,' says Padraic, 'that because of all those changes, I got another nine years out of myself before I finished up. Not only that, but over that time I probably danced better than I had ever danced before.'

Doing it by yourself

If you can't hire a coach, and if you can't find someone willing to coach you for free, you can coach yourself. People have achieved astonishing things on nothing but their own resources.

Self-coaching begins with facing the truth.

Most of us don't have the stomach for this. We don't want to stand in front of a full-length mirror and declare the truth of who we are and where we are. For instance:

'I'm lazy.'

'I'm immature.'

'I don't really believe in myself.'

'I'm fat.'

'I'm living an empty life.'

'I'm petrified at the thought of doing anything different.'

But this is what you need to do. You stand and face yourself and state the truth.

But don't just state it. Write it down. Pour out all of your thoughts and ideas about yourself – every detail, no matter how unpalatable.

Face yourself naked.

If you can't get a coach, ask yourself the hard questions that a coach would ask.

→ Why am I not getting the opportunities I think I deserve?

→ If I continue to behave the way I am, what are the consequences?

→ How committed am I to being the best I can be?

→ Do I want to change? Honestly?

→ In what areas of my life am I accepting mediocrity?

→ When was the last time I pushed myself out of my comfort zone?

→ Am I willing to make the sacrifices required to unlock my potential?

→ What is the biggest thing I am afraid of?

→ Am I growth oriented in *all* aspects of my life?

→ What's the single biggest thing holding me back?

→ Do I spend any time planning my week?

→ Do I work hard enough?

→ Am I eating right?

→ Am I getting enough exercise?

→ Do I spend any time reading?

→ Is my mindset helping me to achieve my potential every day? Or is it stopping me doing so?

Work hard at this. Commit to doing it thoroughly. Ask yourself intelligent, constructive, challenging questions. Questions that will turn you to face the full reality of your life and your lifestyle.

Look back over the things you've done in the past three years.

→ How did you react to opportunities that came along? To crises that arose? To setbacks?

→ Have you been plodding along, doing the same things in the same way all the time?

→ If you had to deal with something new, how did you react to being out of your comfort zone?

→ Did you rush back inside it, or did you learn something from that new experience?

By dissecting all the things that you've done – and those you haven't – you get an understanding of how you think, and how that thinking informs your behaviour. By getting down to the core – by analysing your thinking – you can identify where your mindset is at.

Is it a mindset that allows you to excel? Or is it a mindset that inhibits you?

Is it a mindset that allows you to seek new opportunities? Or is it a mindset that closes off those opportunities?

Your own perspective on your mindset is important, but it shouldn't be the only one. Feedback is vital in breaking down the old ways of thinking.

Even if you are working on your own to develop your mindset, you can benefit from the insights of those around you. Be selective – ask different people to critique different things. For instance:

→ I might ask Padraic Moyles to give me feedback on my physical gestures, my tone of voice, my stage presence.

→ I might get feedback from my dad on content, because he's been studying psychology all his life and has a particular interest in this area.

→ I might ask a friend who is also a teacher about my story-telling. Was the language vivid enough? Was it emotive?

Feedback is a rich resource for someone with a growth mindset. Never, ever think of criticism as attack; think of it as the means by which you can grow, can become more intelligent, more talented than you are.

Don't pull down the shutters against feedback. Reflect on it, dissect it, see what you can use.

3

BUILDING A GROWTH MINDSET

One of the best ways of acquiring a growth mindset is to put yourself in situations where you need one. In McNulty Performance I give the team tasks that have to be completed in a really short space of time. Last year, before our Christmas lunch, I made an announcement.

'We're going to do a twenty-euro challenge. Two teams of five. You've each got €20 and one hour to go out and make a significant difference to someone's life.'

At first, people were resistant. After a great year, I was asking them to do work? At the Christmas party? Why could they not just go on the beer like a normal company?

They got over it. We put the two teams together and off we went.

Team one went to Moore Street, bought a load of roses from the flower sellers there and handed them out free to random people. As you'd expect, they got a wonderful reaction. With the €2 they had left, they went into a fast-food restaurant and leveraged up. They told the staff that they were on a charity challenge but had just €2 left. Could they get ten cups of hot chocolate to give out to homeless people?

The restaurant obliged and the ten cups were handed out to ten grateful recipients.

They came back beaming with pride, feeling great about the impact they had made and all the genuine good feeling they had spread around in that single hour.

I was on team two.

One of the guys, David Simpson, is a veteran of several successful businesses. He said, 'C'mon, we'll go down to the shopping centre, we'll get a cheap hot-water bottle and a big rug and we'll give it to someone who needs it.'

It wasn't a bad idea, but I thought we could do something more. I said, 'Hang on, David, we have to put some thought into this. Let's take a walk and try to come up with something different.'

So we walked in silence for a bit, then I had a thought. I turned to David and said, 'Who do you know?'

'Who do I know? What do you mean, who do I know?'

'Who do you know who could do something for us, who could give us some free product?'

The previous day, we had been on a team building exercise with St Vincent de Paul in their warehouse, sorting out parcels that would go out to families all around Dublin. One thing we had noticed was that there was a lack of gifts for boys aged between fourteen and seventeen. I explained all this to David and his eyes lit up.

'I do know someone, I know a guy who owns a chain of gift shops. I'll call him now.'

So he takes out his phone and calls the guy, who tells him to get down to his shop right away.

Ten minutes later, David's back with two massive bags full of rugby balls, novelty balls, jerseys and T-shirts.

This makes him think of someone else he knows, who runs a shoe shop. So off he goes again.

And this time he comes back with ten boxes of men's shoes.

Meanwhile, I'm in a sports shop trying to score free product from the store manager. He tells me he doesn't have the authority to just give stuff away. Then I remember I know someone in management, so I call him, and put him on the phone to the manager.

Ten minutes later, I'm walking out of there with four bags of sporting goods.

Then another of our colleagues, the Irish Olympian David Gillick, shows up – half an hour late. He couldn't think of anyone he knew in town, so we sent him into a high-end clothes shop and he came back with armloads of blazers and shirts and last season's jeans. By now it was well past the hour, so we headed to the restaurant, where team one was waiting for us.

When they saw us coming in laden down with bags, they couldn't believe it. And when we told them what we had done, they protested, 'But it's all contacts . . . you didn't even spend the money!' And we hadn't – we still had the €20 left (later we did the maths and figured out that we had got about €3,500 worth of gear).

Team one had done well within the bounds of the exercise, but really, the €20 was a distraction. By adopting a growth mindset, we had opened up the exercise to a universe of possibilities, not just those constrained by a meagre twenty euros.

Another example. Just last year, we secured a contract to deliver our Peak Performance programme with Digicel in Papua New Guinea. Getting there wasn't easy. You're talking about two and a half days of travelling, from Dublin to Dubai, then from there to Melbourne and on to Papua New Guinea.

We were going to put 1,200 people through that programme, launching it with a major event the day after we arrived.

The first shock when the minibus pulled up was that there were two guys with guns sitting inside it. We were told that they were our armed guard.

'Armed guard?' I said to our guide. 'Why do we need an armed guard?'

'I can't guarantee your safety without it,' he said.

We were driven to the site where the event was to take place the following day. We had been expecting an arena or a conference venue. What we got was a field. A field and a truck full of equipment. Nothing else.

This was an opportunity to panic. Here we were, jet-lagged and exhausted, supposed to put on our first major event in Papua New Guinea in front of 1,200 people who knew nothing about us, and all we had was a truck full of God-knows-what and an empty field.

We didn't panic.

We decided that somehow, some way, we were going to put together an event that would be world class. It wasn't easy, but we did it.

At half nine the following morning, the field was jammed and the place was rocking.

Take every opportunity to go outside your comfort zone.

For instance, I like to get lost. Head out on the bike, find somewhere I've never been before, then find my way home – without map, GPS or compass, with nothing but my brain.

Try that.

TAKE EVERY OPPORTUNITY TO GO OUTSIDE YOUR COMFORT ZONE.

And think big.

It doesn't matter if you fail, what matters is that you grow.

Think about that twenty-euro challenge. If you had €20 and your job was to make a significant difference to someone's life in the next hour, what would you do?

The world isn't divided into those with a growth mindset and those with a fixed mindset. Most of us have different degrees of both. We frequently meet people who might have exceptional management skills. But ask them about their physical fitness and they have all kinds of explanations for their inability to climb the stairs without having to pause for breath.

Many of us have areas of our lives in which we're stuck, in which we're unwilling to change.

I recently worked with a sportsman whose physical fitness was top class. He understood everything he needed to do in terms of technical skill and execution, rest and recovery, strength and conditioning.

But his attitude to his leadership skills?

'Oh, that's just the way I am,' he would say, 'that's my style.'

Fixed mindset. Apparently immovable.

The wake-up call came in the form of a setback. He missed out on a career-changing opportunity, which left him deeply frustrated. But that piece of adversity was enough to shake him up.

We met up, and discussed what had happened. Then he went off and sought feedback from everyone around him – colleagues in his sport, management and backroom people he worked with. He came back, we sat down and went through the feedback forensically.

At the end of two hours, we had developed a list of concrete steps he could take to adapt his leadership style. Now the thing that was 'just the way I am' was getting radically altered.

You can always change.

Rejecting the accepted wisdom

Reasons *not* to do something are easy to find.

Back when I was trying to make it as a sports psychologist, I ran a gruelling seven-hour training and mental toughness session with an inter-county camogie team. As I was leaving, someone pushed a soggy envelope into my hand. Inside was a voucher worth €30.

Now, if I'd adopted a fixed mindset, I would have asked myself what the hell I was doing with my life. Seven hours' intense work for €30?

With a growth mindset, your view of the world changes. You ask, what is this leading to? So, in this case, I asked myself:

What was the value of that session to my communication skills?

Was I becoming a better coach with sessions like these?

If I could add value to these people's lives, might it lead to something more?

Ultimately, my first corporate gig – with Ulster Bank – came out of pro bono work I'd been doing with the Longford Town soccer team.

I set up my current business in 2005. By 2007, the country had begun to slide into the worst recession any of us had ever seen. Everyone was saying to me, 'Enda, it's time to start thinking about doing something else. Any business you go to will tell you that there's no budget for the kind of work you do.'

I disagreed.

I thought that this was an even bigger opportunity – because companies were going to need the work we did more than ever, if they were going to weather the coming economic storm.

There was nothing revolutionary in my thinking. Any number of companies have got going during downturns. Thomas Edison, the man who invented the light bulb, founded General Electric in 1892. A year later the USA was plunged into a major recession, in which 500 banks closed and 15,000 businesses failed.[3] Revlon Cosmetics was founded in 1932, in the middle of the Great Depression. Microsoft set up in the depths of a recession in 1975. Apple started a year later, and introduced the iPod just after the dot.com bubble had burst in 2001.

A growth mindset transforms the world from one of fixed outcomes and predetermined fates into one bristling with possibility.

I'm *not* saying that you should plunge into something recklessly. Nor am I saying you should delude yourself into continuing to do something that's just not working. I *am* saying look at the situation from all angles.

Don't resign yourself to the accepted wisdom.

---

3 Speaking of Thomas Edison, now there was a man with a growth mindset. A chemist who had just started working for him once asked him about the rules of the laboratory. Edison said: 'Hell, there ain't no rules around here, we're trying to accomplish something!' His relentless pursuit of knowledge and his drive to find better ways of doing things led him to a myriad of discoveries that seem hard to ascribe to a single man. He held over 1,000 patents in the USA, developed what was effectively the world's first research laboratory, and is credited with inventing everything from the phonograph and the motion picture camera to a system for electric power generation and distribution.

Keep your eyes fresh and your mind alive to the possibilities.

Taking action to develop your mindset

A growth mindset requires taking action again, and again, and again. You don't need to feel confident to take action. In fact, chances are you won't feel confident – if you're adopting a growth mindset, you're taking on something new and challenging. Remember that you can't know you're not good at something until you put in the effort and find out. So, it doesn't matter that you're not confident, it only matters that you take action.

Similarly, feeling bad is no reason to curl up and die. If something has gone wrong, if you've suffered a setback, let it be a spur. It doesn't matter how you feel, so long as you act to improve things.

For people with a growth mindset, the worse they feel, the greater their drive to make things better.

Taking action can be daunting, and daunting things are easy to put off. Don't focus on the thousands of things you'd like to do, focus on the one thing you have to do.

Suppose you've sent in a CV to a company you'd really like to work for. Follow up on it with a call. Commit to a concrete action, one that you can visualize: 'This afternoon, just after lunch, I'm going to find a quiet room, get my notes prepared and call.'

Or suppose your CV didn't make the cut, and you get a rejection letter. Don't let that experience become a failure, make it work for you instead. Try to find out why your CV was rejected. Call them up, ask to speak to the personnel manager, or whoever signed the letter. Be polite, of course, and direct and clear.

What was wrong with your application?

Maybe nothing. Maybe they're just not hiring now.

Or maybe you'll find out where your CV was weak – maybe you'll find out what areas you need to develop in order to be considered next time.

Maybe the act of making that call will be remembered as an act of initiative – maybe you'll get the inside track the next time the company is hiring.

Carol Dweck talks about the transformative power of thinking in terms of 'Yet'. In her TED talk, 'The Power of Believing You Can Improve', she says:

> 'If you get a failing grade, you think, I'm nothing, I'm nowhere. But if you get the grade 'Not Yet' you understand that you're on a learning curve. It gives you a path into the future.'

She goes on to describe an online maths challenge, created in conjunction with scientists from the University of Washington, in which students who participated were rewarded for effort, strategy and progress, as opposed to the usual rewards for getting an immediate right answer. The researchers found that students rewarded in this way put in more effort, were engaged with the exercise over longer periods of time, and demonstrated perseverance when they hit tougher problems.

REJECTION IS NOT A JUDGEMENT ON YOU – UNLESS YOU DECIDE IT IS.

Remember that rejection is not a judgement on you. Unless you decide it is.

Something that seemed like a failure might give you valuable information if you examine it carefully.

Think about something from your past that went wrong. It might be a relationship breakdown, a loss at sport, an interview that you flunked, a disaster at work. Pick one of these.

Picture everything that happened.

Now, think about it with a growth mindset. Look at it dispassionately, not with yourself as the victim or the loser or the wronged party.

What did you learn from it?

Is there something in that experience you can use to help you grow?

Why you need to mind your mindset

When a crisis hits, you see what a growth mindset really looks like. It's the ability to rise, hold a hand up and bring the panic and fear to a halt. And then to look at the crisis dispassionately and choose a response.

Suppose someone was to walk into my office right now and say, 'Enda, we've just lost ten contracts.'

What do I do? How do I react?

What I should be asking myself is, what is the right mindset at this point? Which is the mindset that will allow me to handle this situation best as a leader?

We'll be dealing with that response in more detail in Chapter 10, 'Resilience in action'. For now, it's enough to know that changing your mindset is not a matter of flicking a switch. It is a process, not a one-off action. It's about having worked on and developed practices that allow you to switch into the right mindset when it's really needed.

Holding on to a growth mindset requires constant monitoring. You must monitor your thoughts, your attitudes, your reactions.

The human brain is buzzing with a dozen different thoughts and stresses and idle daydreams. This mental babble distances us from our lives. It makes it hard to focus on whatever we're supposed to be doing.

You're talking to someone but you're not absorbing what they're saying, or how they're saying it.

Your eyes might be following a line of text but your brain is off somewhere else, and nothing is going in.

You can eat an entire meal without tasting it.

You can look at something without seeing it.

Sometimes zoning out isn't a big deal; you slip into autopilot on your morning commute and get to work without being aware of the details of the journey. But if you don't call a halt to this constant mental chatter, your life passes you by. You don't remember anything, because you weren't present while it was happening.

A recent study published in the journal *Psychological Science* looked at the impact of this phenomenon on creative thinking. The experiments involved giving participants a free-association task – each was given a word and had to respond as quickly as possible with the first word that came to mind. At the same time, the researchers handed participants an additional task – half of the group had to remember a two-digit number, while the other half had to remember a seven-digit number.

The researchers found that the participants who were trying to retain the long string of numbers responded to the free-association exercise in less imaginative ways than those who had to remember just two numbers. The former group gave statistically common answers (e.g. 'white' / 'black') while those whose brains weren't as heavily taxed came up with more creative responses to the same word (e.g. 'white' / 'cloud').

The point here is that the mind's running commentary on your life – that endless loop of thought and worry and self-talk – gets in the way of the real business of life. It stops you from thinking creatively, from engaging with what you want to do.

It's so easy to get sucked into the chaos and minutiae of everyday life, and to slip back into bad habits. You need almost constant awareness of your mindset. Real-time awareness.

How am I thinking right now? At this exact moment?

Am I absorbing what I'm reading here?

Am I open to all of the possibilities that are flowing past?

Am I doing everything I can to grow and move forward?

If you struggle with managing your mind, meditation can be a wonderful resource. There are few things as powerful for anchoring you in the present and giving your mind the freedom to concentrate on what's real, on what you actually want to do.

Becoming your true self

The process of exploring how you think – and how it may be impeding your growth – isn't just about the pursuit of material success. The growth mindset is a powerful tool for revealing the flaws in your thinking and allowing you to become a fuller, more authentic version of yourself.

A few years ago, I was invited into a large, Dublin-based multinational to do a one-off motivation session for one of their sales teams. Afterwards I went for a coffee with the

Sales Manager, AnnMarie Phillips. Throughout her career, AnnMarie had been working for blue-chip companies in what they call FMCG – Fast-Moving Consumer Goods. She had just come back after her second maternity leave and was now being pulled in two directions. Somewhere along the line, between motherhood and career, she had lost sight of her sense of purpose, of what she was all about and what she wanted. She felt that she wasn't in control of her future.

I agreed to give her some mentoring to help her make the changes she needed to make.

During our first ninety-minute meeting, we did a mind-mapping exercise. We talked about:

What was important in her life?

Who was important in her life?

Where did she get her energy from?

What did she want to achieve?

And, crucially, what was stopping her from achieving her goals?

That process of asking these questions – exploring why we think what we think – that, in itself, can be an energizing experience. So much of the time, we do what we do without thinking about it.

For AnnMarie, starting the process of examining her life was illuminating.

'I remember driving away from that meeting and feeling that the lights had been turned on. Having drifted for so long, I now had a sense of where I was. Over the next year or so, we met irregularly – perhaps once every two or three months. But each time, Enda asked me very challenging questions – uncomfortable questions that I hadn't been asking myself, and challenging my beliefs about my world, about what I took to be real . . . about everything, really.'

Realizing that there is such a thing as a growth mindset launches you on the road towards adopting one.

One of the big breakthroughs AnnMarie made was making the connection between who she was at work and who she was at home. She began to realize that the more fulfilled you are in one area of your life, the more fulfilled you can be in another. You're just the one person, always. Dividing yourself up to become one persona at work and another at home creates a kind of disequilibrium in your life that makes it difficult to be your best self in either role.

'That was something that I struggled with. I was a mother to two young kids, and I was also trying to build a career. These two things had become separated in my mind. What coaching made me realize is that actually having faith in myself and calling out what I wanted, then working towards it, that was the right way to go. And then just showing up like that person, that was really powerful.'

Acquiring a growth mindset is such an energizing experience that you want everyone to know about it. AnnMarie turned the spotlight on her own leadership style and began to think about how she could use what she had discovered about herself with her sales teams.

'Now I ask those uncomfortable, probing questions and encourage the people I work with to dig deeper and self-reflect. Once it's clear that I want each member of my team to become more fulfilled – not just in their working lives but in everything they do – they respond very positively. Each one of them has remarked on how different I've become over the last couple of years since I launched this mentoring process. They're seeing the real me. I'm much happier, I'm much more relaxed.'

AnnMarie has since been promoted to Sales Director for one of the largest parts of the business, and the business itself has had its best two years in a long time.

'A lot of it is to do with the belief that I have in myself and that I have in my team. I believe in creating conditions for people to be themselves, to help them to create possibilities for the future, to build an attitude that fosters a growth mindset and takes enjoyment in what they do. Nothing seems impossible now. I *know* when I'm at my best and what it takes to keep me in that space. I might not have all the answers, but I believe in the possibility and that we can find a way to do amazing things for the business and ourselves.

'Mentoring made that link for me. It showed me that *I* was at the centre, and my personal life and my work life were around me, whereas I was disassociating the three. But when you're true to yourself, you're so much more aware of how you show up and the impact you have on others.'

MINDSET – TAKE ACTION NOW!

1. *Examine a recent setback.* Look at it with a fixed mindset. Now look at it with a growth mindset. What does it teach you about yourself? How can you use that lesson?

2. *Make a list of all of the people who might be willing to give you feedback on some aspect of your performance.* Now call them up and ask them to give you comprehensive feedback.

3. *Look at some of the hard questions detailed in these three chapters.* Pick one aspect of your life. It can be anything – exercise, dealing with a difficult colleague at work, something you've identified as a weakness – and decide that this week you will adopt a growth mindset in relation to it.

4. *Do one thing today that will put you outside your comfort zone.* Feel the discomfort – don't rush back inside. Use the experience to open your mind to possibilities. Think differently about yourself.

5. *Do one thing each day over the next ninety days that requires a growth mindset.* Perhaps take a different route to work. Perhaps write with your left hand. Do a sport or activity that you never did before. Read a book about astrophysics. Go someplace you've never been before.

MISSION

4

MEANING

There's a huge amount of information and advice out there about the importance of setting goals and how to follow them, and that's all great. But before you begin, you need to ask yourself a fundamental question.

What do you want to achieve? I mean *really* want to achieve?

The main reason people give up on goals is that they're not meaningful enough for them. So when you consider the answer, the most important thing to think about – perhaps the *only* important thing – is meaning.

Whatever your goal is, it must be meaningful.

A meaningful goal is central to who you are. It is aligned to your purpose in life, your reason for existing. If you were to strip away all the other characteristics of a goal and were left with meaning alone, that – arguably – would be enough to carry you through.

Identifying a meaningful goal is about the 'why' of your life. You want to achieve a goal for a reason. What is that reason – the 'why'?

The 'why' needs to be huge. If you have a big enough 'why', you'll find a way.

In spring 1800, Napoleon was looking for a way to get through to Italy, which was in the control of the Austrians, and retake it for France. The key to his planned strategy was surprise. It was believed that the St Bernard Pass through the Alps was unnavigable during the spring. As a result, it was left unguarded by the Austrians. So Napoleon chose to go that way. He is reputed to have said, 'There will be no Alps.'

One problem was transporting heavy artillery through deep snow. His solution was to have it all disassembled and packed into crates; the barrels of the guns were carried in hollow fir trees. Once the army had made it through, the artillery was reassembled and Napoleon led his troops to victory at Marengo.

I watched Paul O'Connell closely while working with the Irish rugby team. No matter what the context – in meetings, on the training pitch, in rehabilitation sessions, in scrummaging sessions and, of course, in the games themselves – everything he did was done to the best of his ability. While others might flag in the last five minutes, or the last five metres, he kept going with the same relentless intensity. How he spoke, how he brought players with him, how he dealt with pain – everything about him communicated the same relentless mindset. He never stopped trying to be better, right up until the day he retired.

Why?

Because O'Connell's mission had a meaning, a 'why' that was almost tangible. He wanted to be the best, and nothing would get in his way in pursuit of that.

Before I got anywhere near the Armagh County panel, I spent eight years working my ass off to get on it. To get us to an All-Ireland title took immense dedication from a wide variety of people, all of whom wanted that title more than anything else in the world. The coaches, the senior players, the guys on the county board, the fringe players – the guys who never got any credit – put in ten years of work. We put everything else in our lives on hold in pursuit of this goal.

For ten years I drove two hours, three or four nights a week, to Armagh, getting back to Dublin at 12.30 a.m., driving through busy streets, looking out at all the throngs of people our age going to nightclubs. I was heading home to bed wrecked. I never once thought of parking the car and going off on the tear. Then there were the gym sessions, the physio sessions, the early mornings, the video work, the pool sessions, the preparation before games, the mental training sessions, the speed sessions, the rehabilitation sessions after the numerous injuries, the constant attention to what I ate.

I and every other guy on the squad did that – day in, day out.

I remember recovery sessions at an equine therapy centre in Co. Louth, where we immersed ourselves in freezing water for what felt like hours – and I'm allergic to horses. Driving out of there, red-eyed and sneezing, I could barely see.

We knocked lumps out of each other in tackling sessions. One night, one of my best friends, Paul McGrane, accidentally head-butted me and split me open just below my eye (I still have the scar). I was told to go to the hospital, get stitched up and get back on the pitch. When we were changing afterwards, the only sympathy from Paul was an offhand inquiry, 'How's the eye?' If the situation had been reversed, I'm sure I would have been exactly the same.

That was the mindset that we built in Armagh. That was how we lived, that's how we achieved what we achieved.

Nowadays, when I look at the successful teams that we work with, I recognize elements of the culture we had in

Armagh at that time. I recognize the same type of leadership, that same underlying ethos.

Why was it there?

Because of our motivation, our meaning.

We wanted to win an All-Ireland and were prepared to put everything on the line in the service of that goal.

Meaning is the gravitational pole that draws everything to it. Where there is meaning, all of the effort and pain and struggle disintegrates and ultimately disappears.

SUCCESS WITHOUT FULFILMENT IS FAILURE.

Remember too that success without fulfilment is failure. This is the sinking feeling you experience when you achieve the goal, but you look at it and go, 'What was that about? Why did I want to achieve that?'

I once decided that what I wanted to do was buy four properties in four cities by 2006. And I did it. But the lack of any sense of accomplishment once I had them left me bewildered.

I realized that I didn't want four properties in four cities. It was a meaningless goal.

I had a guy in the office yesterday who works for one of our clients. His title is Head of Mischief. His job is to create marketing campaigns that push the boundaries of audacity and creativity. His passion for his work lights up the room when he talks about it. He loves what he does.

What about you? Do you love what you do?

Remember, you will spend far more of your life at work than you will with your family and friends. It needs to be worth it.

The best people in all walks of life – and I'm not talking about famous people here, I'm talking about the best teachers, the best engineers, the best mechanics, the best journalists – are passionate about what they do. They don't do it for the money. Status or fame don't matter. It's all about the passion.

Meaning is the source of the passion, and passion is what will sustain you in the journey towards your mission.

If you set a goal but you're not passionate about it, why the hell would you stick to it? If your mission is infused with meaning, it's like a goal on steroids. It is much more powerful.

If you mean it, write it down

Anybody can set spur-of-the-moment goals – there for as long as they take to dream up, then forgotten and gone. If you're serious about this, your goals will be with you for a long time.

Real goals have got to be considered carefully. They have to be compelling. Ultimately, what you are doing is designing a mission. Goals are the navigational points that lead you towards that mission.

Work backwards from your desired destination.

If your mission is to change career, your goals will reflect the fact that you need to:

→ go back to college,
→ find a mentor to help you acquire the new skills you need, and
→ save money to make this happen.

If your mission is to build a game-changing company, your goals will map out the incremental steps you need to achieve that:

→ getting seed capital,

→ finding premises,

→ registering the company, and

→ building a brand.

Write up a draft, think about it, get feedback on it, get a mentor or someone you trust to interrogate your thinking. Then rethink, redraft . . . and repeat.

You must write down your goals. If you don't write them down, how can you review them? How can you tell if they're detailed enough? How can you get somebody else to review them with you?

Once you're clear on meaning and mission, use the SMARTER acronym to help you nail down those goals with greater precision and clarity. SMARTER goals are Specific, Measurable, Action orientated, Realistic, Time bound, Exciting and Reviewable.

→ *Specific*
Do you want a rewarding job that pays well and gives you Fridays off to spend with your children? Do you want to earn a salary of €100,000 within the next two years? Do you want to play for a provincial rugby side within the next three years? Do you want to run a business with an operating profit of €2,000,000? 'I'm going to climb mountains' is a vague ambition, not a goal. 'I'm going to climb Kilimanjaro with five of my friends by June 2018' is a goal. Nail it down so that there's no ambiguity about whether or not you've accomplished your mission.

→ *Measurable*
Nothing happens overnight. You need to be able to gauge your progress towards your mission continuously.

Make sure you can identify the intermediate steps that indicate how you're progressing. Experience has shown that the people who set measurable goals are much more likely to achieve them.

→ *Action orientated*

No goal will ever be met unless you take action. Every goal must involve positive, focused action.

→ *Realistic*

Is it realistic that Enda McNulty will be the best opera singer in the world? Maybe not. Is it realistic that he grows his company so that it's turning over €10 million within three years? Maybe it is. While your goal has got to stretch you, it must also obey the laws of physics.

→ *Time bound*

Put a date on it.

→ *Exciting*

Where is this goal coming from? Is it a goal your boss has set you? Is it a goal your mother has set you? Does she want you to become a doctor? That's your mother's goal, not yours. What's going to happen in five years' time when you're flat out between studying and hospital work, and none of it means a thing to you. Stop. Now. If you're not passionate about your goal, you won't stick at it.

→ *Reviewable*

Your goals document is a living document. I carry mine in a Moleskine diary, I have it in my phone and on my tablet. My goals are branded into my brain. You review constantly, so that you know where you are and how you're progressing. Reviewing your goals is not just about knowing where you are. Remember what you're trying to do here. You are trying to change things. You are trying to create something new. Constant repetition and focus on your goals is primarily about reprogramming your mind, replacing old habits with new ones.

The moon-shot

Yes, your mission has to obey the laws of physics, but I am also convinced that some goals should be outlandish. Some goals should be set to excite you, to inspire you, to stir you, to challenge every single cell in your body.

When the Wright brothers set out to build an aeroplane, was that goal realistic?

When NASA was charged with finding a way to fly to the moon, I've no doubt there was someone in the back of the room who said, 'Hang on there, lads, we should really try to come up with a more realistic target here.'

I've been in a lot of rooms like that.

In launching the original moon-shot goal, John F. Kennedy said, 'We choose to go to the moon in this decade and do the other things, not because they are easy, but because they are hard.'

In the spring of 1916, Ernest Shackleton and his crew became stranded on Elephant Island in the South Atlantic after their ship, *Endurance*, was crushed by the ice. Shackleton, accompanied by Tom Crean – arguably the greatest team player in Irish history – set out on one of the most daring missions ever undertaken at sea. Sailing an open boat – the *James Caird* – across 800 nautical miles of stormy, treacherous, sub-Antarctic oceans, they reached South Georgia in sixteen days, having fought storms, huge seas and freezing conditions. Once they landed, they had to

cross the frozen, mountainous interior of the island –
something which no one had ever done before. This would
have been a tall order in any circumstances, but after sixteen
days fighting the South Atlantic, and with the most rudimen-
tary supplies and equipment, it represented an overwhelming
challenge.

Yet, thirty-six hours later, Shackleton, Crean and the ship's
captain, Frank Worsley, made it to the whaling station on the
far side of the island. The station chief had met Shackleton
eighteen months earlier, but he didn't recognize the filthy,
bedraggled man who showed up, seemingly out of nowhere,
at 3 p.m. that afternoon.

Setting out for South Georgia was anything but a
SMARTER goal. It was wild, audacious and borderline crazy,
but that is what they had to do to survive. Realistically, they
were doomed to either starve or freeze to death. But because
of their daring and courage, every member of the party –
those stranded on Elephant Island and those who went for
help – survived.

The man in the yellow sports car who dreamed of climbing mountains

Ian McKeever was another man who didn't look at the world
in quite the same way as the rest of us. I first heard of Ian
through my good friend, the former Armagh footballer Des
Mackin. Des called me up one day and asked me if I'd meet
Ian.

'He's a DJ in town,' he told me, 'and he's got this crazy
goal.'

'Go on.'

'He wants to climb the seven highest mountains in the world in world-record time.'

'Wow. Right. So he's a mountain climber.'

'No. He went up Carrauntoohil once.'

'But he's in good shape, right?'

'Well, no. He's not that fit.'

'But he has a good team behind him, right?'

'Ah,' says Des, 'that's where you come in. He wants you to be part of his team.'

I agreed to meet Ian the following Saturday morning in a coffee shop in Dun Laoghaire. Des and I were there first to talk through the plan – such as it was – in a little more detail. While we were talking, there was a commotion at the door and this guy burst into the place. He was wearing an old pair of jeans, white runners, a worn-out blazer and sported a mop of peroxide hair. Talk about a bundle of energy. He bounced from table to table, chatting to everyone, laughing, joking.

'Enda,' said Des, 'meet Ian.'

When he eventually joined us, Ian threw open his arms and said, 'I want to break the world record. I want to climb the seven highest mountains in the world faster than anyone else has ever done it.'

I quizzed him about his experience (very little), his physical fitness (also very little) and his nutrition (not so hot either). Ian was honest about these things. But despite his utter lack of preparation and experience, he was still committed to this crazy goal. The more I questioned him, the more he smiled, and the more infectious his enthusiasm became. That enthusiasm, that zest for life, that unshakeable commitment – anyone could see there was something special in that. He knew, however, that he couldn't do it on enthusiasm alone. He knew he needed help.

'If you really want to do this, you're going to have to live and breathe it,' I said to him. 'You're talking about some serious mental and physical graft. Are you up for that?'

He jumped up, rattling against the table and nearly spilling my coffee. 'Yeah, I'm up for that. But I'm on the radio in half an hour. Gotta go.'

He was out the door in half a second. Then we heard the roar of an engine, the toot of a car horn, and something sleek and yellow accelerated past the window.

I phoned him later in the week, and we agreed to start training that Saturday at 8 a.m. in Glendalough.

Des and I were there first. Eight o'clock came, then ten past eight. Then twenty past. At half eight, a bright yellow sports car skidded into the place and screeched to a halt in front of us. Ian erupted out of the car, which was packed to the gills with climbing equipment – bags, boots, ice axes, ropes, carabiners – everything you can think of.

As he disentangled himself from a rope, I was thinking to myself that there was no way this guy would ever be organized enough to climb Everest, let alone any of the other peaks. In record time? Not a chance.

Des and I had worked out a plan for that first morning. We had decided that we would try and break him. We would push him so hard that he would give in, throw up his arms and say, 'That's it, I'm finished, I can't do any more.'

It sounds harsh, but we knew that there was every chance he was going to be physically and mentally broken on the side of one of those mountains. If we broke him now, he would have to build himself back up. And then, when it happened in the 'Death Zone' on Everest, he'd be ready for it. He would know how to respond.

Des and I had taken the whole day off to focus on this, and we had estimated that by about the third hour, Ian would be ready to throw in the towel.

So we began, nice and gently, with a few easy challenges – lifting logs, running uphill with a weighted rucksack on his back . . .

Sixteen minutes.

That's all it took. He broke after sixteen minutes. He pulled a muscle behind his knee and couldn't do any more. He sank to the ground, his head hanging between his knees, defeated.

We left him alone for ten minutes, then came back and laid it on the line.

'Ian, you're fooling yourself. Your plan is a joke. Physically, you're nowhere near where you have to be. Mentally, you're nowhere near strong enough. You're not ready for Glendalough, let alone Everest.'

Ian didn't look at me as I said all this. He sat there staring at the ground. Then he stood up and, without another word, he limped to his car, got in and drove away.

He phoned me up about a week later.

'You're right,' he said, 'I need to get serious about this. I need to get, you know, professional. Because basically I'm bluffing. That's what I'm doing, I'm bluffing. But that's over, I'm ready to start, I'm ready to commit.'

And that's how the real work started. We put together a master plan on an Excel spreadsheet on Ian's battered laptop. This plan covered everything from nutrition and physical conditioning to mental preparation, funding and business planning, logistics and communications, and PR.

Nothing was left to chance.

I can't say Ian became the ultimate pro, but he committed to the plan. He worked very hard and made huge leaps in his physical and mental conditioning. And anything he lacked in physical terms, he made up for in self-belief and persistence. He had so much belief in himself, the fact that he wasn't in prime condition almost became secondary. And what's more, he made sure to surround himself with a very strong team.

And he did it. He reached his goal.

In 2007, he climbed all seven peaks in 155 days – the fastest anyone had ever done it before.

Was this a SMARTER goal?

Not even close. It was wildly, stupidly ambitious.

How did he do it?

He started with that moon-shot goal and worked backwards.

If I'm going to climb seven of the world's highest mountains in five months, I'm going to have to get really fit – *that's doable*.

If I'm going to climb the world's highest mountains in five months, I'm going to have to prepare mentally – *doable too*.

If I'm going to climb the world's highest mountains in five months, I'm going to have to achieve a set of financial and logistical goals – *all doable*.

By breaking that insane goal down into bite-size chunks, it suddenly became sane.

And once that plan was made, Ian got busy every single day, making it happen.

The thought of Everest was especially daunting. 'I just can't get my head around it,' he said to me. 'I can visualize the other peaks, but Everest? I just can't get my head around it.'

A couple of years earlier, I had travelled to the World Athletics Championships in Osaka with David Gillick. I'd been interested in Buddhism for some time, and while in Japan the thing I most wanted to do was to meet a Buddhist monk.

At first, I hit a lot of dead ends. I was told that the tradition had died out near Osaka, that there were no monks left. But eventually, someone knew someone, who knew someone else, who knew of a small community living in the mountains not too far from where we were staying. One of those monks agreed to meet us, so David and I and a few of the other Irish athletes travelled out there one morning and spent a day with the monk and his family.

It was a wonderful, eye-opening experience. There was a quietness about the place that could not have contrasted more with the chaos of downtown Osaka. The monk welcomed us in and taught us a range of meditation rituals that I still use today. In fact, those few hours we spent with him were among the most enriching and useful I have ever spent.

Anyway, when Ian started explaining how daunted he felt by Everest, I talked him through a walking meditation ritual that I learned that day. It was based around a technique called 'One breath, one step'. The idea is that taking one breath is easy. So is taking one step. Combining the two allowed Ian to take an Everest-sized challenge and deconstruct it into something that was achievable.

Tragically, Ian was killed by a lightning strike on Mount Kilimanjaro in January 2013.

I think about him every day. I tell his story to so many of the teams and the organizations we work with. I think of what he used to say: 'You'll never be famous as an explorer until you're dead.'

Ian's achievement continues to serve as an inspiration for so many people. He proved just how far you can get with a good plan and a lot of self-belief.

He proved too that you don't have to be a superhero, that these moon-shot goals – crazy as they seem – can be reached, and by anyone.

YOU DON'T HAVE TO BE A SUPERHERO – MOON-SHOT GOALS CAN BE REACHED BY ANYONE.

OK, so some goals *have* to be SMARTER.

In my business this week, the team and I need to have SMARTER goals. We have to ensure that we deliver a certain amount of billable hours each month. But we've also got some ludicrously ambitious goals. Our vision is to be a game-changing company that transforms human potential globally. That's not exactly a SMARTER goal, but there is a clear alignment between those smaller navigational points and our larger vision.

You've got to dream bigger, and name the one thing you want above all others.

Once it's meaningful, once you're passionate about it, that vision will sustain you through all of the other smaller, SMARTER navigational points along the way.

5

NAME IT

There's a special power in declaring what you are going to do in front of witnesses. You've got to say it, you've got to name it. Declare it in the open, take responsibility for whatever it is you want to do.

Put it out there and commit to it.

Back in 1999, Armagh had won the Ulster Championship for the first time in years, and we were playing Meath in the All-Ireland semi-final. The match was like a talented young boxer (us) going up against a wily old one (Meath).

During the match I heard the Meath manager, Sean Boylan, tell the man I was marking, 'Take him out to middle of the field.' So off he went. And naively I followed him out from corner back, thereby creating acres of space inside for the forwards to run into. Next thing, my long-time teammate Ger Reid pulled his man down to prevent a certain goal. Ger got a red card.

We lost that match by four points. The scoreline could have been worse. We were too inexperienced, we weren't ready for the occasion.

We didn't know how to win in Croke Park in front of 80,000 people . . . *yet*.

Despair comes like an avalanche after a defeat like that. Months and months of unwavering dedication and hard, hard work get torn apart in a matter of minutes.

We all returned to our clubs to try to pick up the pieces.

Then, about six weeks later, someone called a players' meeting in the Canal Court Hotel in Newry. It was evening and the room was poorly lit – or at least, that's how I remember it. Our mood was sombre, gloomy almost. When anyone stood up to speak, there was precious little positivity or optimism in what they said. We were supposed to be planning, but we just couldn't seem to get out from under that defeat.

Then Tony McEntee stood up to speak. He was one of the most respected leaders on the team, and when he spoke – in a hard-edged Crossmaglen accent – he combined a kind of steely gravitas with real energy and conviction. He sugar-coated nothing.

'Listen, guys,' he said, 'if this team doesn't win the All-Ireland, it'll be an absolute joke. It will be a shame. A disgrace. We need to be thinking about winning the All-Ireland. This team should be thinking about nothing else.'

It may not sound that earth-shattering now, but no one had ever declared that ambition in front of the entire team before. Sure, we'd talked about it at the bar over a bottle of beer, or someone on the team might have said that we were good enough to beat Kerry, or beat Meath, or beat Galway. But no one had stood up in that context and drawn that responsibility out into the open.

If we don't win the All-Ireland, it will be a disgrace.

I can't remember anything else from the meeting. I can't remember much about the next six months, but I remember that moment vividly. The steel in his voice, the belief in his eyes.

Putting the goal out there was a vital step on the road to winning the All-Ireland three years later.

Tell someone

Here's a common pitfall. You set goals in a rush of enthusiasm, only to forget them when that enthusiasm flags.

A great way to keep yourself on track is to share those goals.

A study conducted in 2015 by the Department of Psychology in the Dominican University of California tells us a lot about the value of setting clear, written goals, then getting someone else to help you keep your promises to yourself. They recruited 267 participants and randomly assigned them to one of five groups.

Group 1 was asked to *think* about business-related goals they hoped to accomplish within a four-week block and to rate each goal according to:

→ difficulty,
→ importance,
→ the extent to which they had the skills and resources to accomplish the goal,
→ their commitment and motivation, and
→ whether they had pursued the goal before – and if so, how they got on.

Groups 2–5 were asked to *write down* their goals and then rate them using the same criteria.

Group 3 was asked to write down their goals *and* action commitments for each goal.

Group 4 had to write down goals and action commitments *and* share these commitments with someone else.

Group 5 went the furthest by doing all of the above *plus* sending a weekly progress report to a friend.

The goals chosen were quite wide ranging, and included everything from completing a project and increasing income to reducing work anxiety and learning a new skill. Specific goals ranged from writing a chapter of a book to selling a house.

Of the original 267 participants, 149 completed the study. These participants were asked to rate their progress and the degree to which they had accomplished their goals. At the end of the study, 43% of Group 1 had either accomplished their goals or were at least halfway there, while 62% of Group 4 had either accomplished their goals or were more than halfway there. However, 76% of those in Group 5 had either accomplished their goals or were at least halfway towards accomplishing them.

The lesson is clear.

When you set out to achieve a goal, having an 'accountability partner' makes the possibility of success that much higher. Whether it's your boss, your best friend, your husband, your mother, your father, your friend in school.

HAVING AN 'ACCOUNTABILITY PARTNER' MAKES THE POSSIBILITY OF SUCCESS THAT MUCH HIGHER.

You need someone who'll ring you up and say, 'OK, Enda, where are you at with your sales? Talk me through your operating profit this month.'

Or who will ask, 'How many weights sessions did you get to last week? How's your nutrition, or how is your mental training?'

Or who will tell you, 'You haven't had a holiday in two years. How the hell are you going to achieve your goals without some rest and recovery time?'

It's someone who'll offer to support you: 'You need to get exercise. I'll meet you in the park at three and we'll do a half-hour walk with the kids in their strollers.'

Whatever it is, whatever you've committed to do, getting someone else involved keeps you honest. It makes it far more likely that you'll do what you set out to do.

Anticipate setbacks

Expect things to go wrong. Expect the illness that knocks you out of your fitness routine, the loss of a contract that plunges your business into disaster, the sudden crisis that turns your world upside down.

Expect it. Because it's going to happen.

I learned this lesson very young. When I was seventeen years old, I broke my arm so badly that I was told I would never play football again. Talk about a setback? All I had ever wanted – the only thing I thought about – was playing football.

It was a beautiful summer's evening, and my brothers and cousins and I were taking in hay. We were bringing it back home from my uncle's farm, a distance of about seven miles. We had his battered old tractor and trailer, and the intention was to take the load over the mountains. This wasn't hard agricultural labour – we just wanted to take the hay in for fun. So we piled it high on top of the trailer and tied it down with ropes as best we could. Then the boys all climbed on top and I set off driving.

I took her slow and steady along the Flagstaff Road, listening to the shouts and laughter up on top of the hay. We stopped off at the first shop we came to. The boys all climbed down, we went into the shop and stocked up on sweets and soft drinks. At this point, I'd had enough of driving. All the fun was up on top.

I said, 'Right, guys, I've driven most of the way, now it's my turn up there.'

Nobody would agree to drive.

But I wouldn't let it go. 'I'll say it again. I drove three-quarters of the way, now someone else drive the rest of the way. I want a bit of craic on top.'

So eventually my brother Justin said, 'Right, grand, I'll drive.'

Great. The rest of us climbed up on top of the load, and off we went again.

There's a straight road out from the village for about a quarter of a mile, then you come to a T-junction. I recall thinking, as we approached that junction, *he's going too fast*. I was listening to the sound of the engine, waiting for the revs to ease off, but they never did. Through the laughing and joking and messing up on top of the hay, I remember a small, insistent worm of a thought. *We're in danger here.*

Then we hit the T-junction, Justin braked and the trailer flipped.

We were all tossed up into the air as if we were in zero gravity. I remember everything happening almost in slow motion. I remember rising up through the air and looking up at a shower of multicoloured sweets – yellows and purples and reds – rising above me and then falling with me.

There was a house at the T-junction, with a ranch-style fence to the front. As I fell, my arm came scything down through that fence. I landed on my back and knew straight away that I was in serious trouble. I could see my forearm was mangled. The agony of it. Almost immediately, it blew up like a balloon.

Next thing, people were running screaming from the house.

Justin was in shock. He was lying there moaning, 'What the hell? What the hell is going on?'

There were bales of sodden hay everywhere. My cousins were picking themselves up off the ground – they were sore and hobbling, but they were OK.

But my arm. My arm was smashed.

I passed out in the ambulance and was taken first to Daisy Hill Hospital in Newry, then to the Royal Victoria in Belfast where they tried to put my arm back together. Of all the hospitals that I could have been brought to, this was probably the best. The surgeons there were used to dealing with bomb victims, and guys who had their limbs smashed in punishment beatings.

I remember the surgeon coming in with the X-rays. He held them defensively, as if he didn't want me to see them.

'There are multiple fractures,' he told me, 'and very significant neural damage.' Then he lowered one X-ray and showed it to me.

My arm was a mess. There were bits of bone everywhere.

They ended up having to insert a plate along the top of the forearm, and a plate along the bottom, with multiple screws going in at all kinds of odd angles, trying to find a bit of bone to anchor into. I can still feel them there today.

I told the surgeon I was a footballer. And at the time, I wanted to be a physiotherapist.

He took a deep breath. 'Your right arm is in bad shape. It's not good. It's unlikely you'll ever use it properly again.'

I left the hospital three weeks later with my arm in a sling, unable to move any of my fingers. They'd put it in a splint, with a series of elastic bands holding my fingers open so that my hand wouldn't close up for good.

I became seriously depressed. My dream had been to play football, and now that was gone. I loved training, but I couldn't even jog.

I went back to school in September. I was so depressed, I was barely present. I withdrew into myself.

Three months went by without any movement in my hand.

I was heading into biology one afternoon when the teacher, Gerry Hughes, stopped and asked me what the matter was. His wife was one of my mother's best friends, and he himself was a great teacher. Charismatic, fun, irreverent – a total maverick. Everyone loved his classes.

'It's this arm, sir,' I said, 'I can't move it, I'll never move it again. My football career's over. I'm devastated, sir.'

He brought me into the room behind the biology lab, where the technicians worked. He sat me down and got me to take off the sling and lay my arm out on the big mahogany workbench – like a biological specimen.

It looked like something dead. The muscle had atrophied, the skin was yellow and purple. You could see the screws pushing up against the skin.

'Who told you you'll never move it again?'

'The surgeon. He said I have to start trying to write with my left hand.'

'What's this surgeon's name?'

I told him.

Gerry made a face. Then he said, 'I want you to listen to me, and listen to me carefully.' He brought his fist down on the bench. 'First of all, you don't be worrying about the surgeon. Forget him.'

'What?'

'Forget what he told you. What I want you to do is work that hand. From now on, I want you to work that hand every single day.'

He took out a 2p coin and he put it on the table. 'Push that,' he said, 'with your thumb.'

I turned my arm over so that my thumb was at the edge of the coin and I tried to move it, but I couldn't. 'I can't, I can't do it.'

'You can't today,' he said. 'But try again tomorrow, and keep trying until you can. Now. Has the surgeon sent you to an occupational therapist yet?'

'A what?'

He rolled his eyes. 'An occupational therapist is like a physio, only he'll be able to help you with your hand more specifically. Get back up to Daisy Hill today, tell them who you are, what happened to you. And tell them you need an OT.'

So that afternoon, I went back up to the hospital and met an occupational therapist.

Within a couple of days, she had started me on a rehabilitation programme. One of the first exercises I had to do involved moving this little clothes peg – the spring in it was so weak a baby could have opened it – from one sheet of paper to another. There were another ten or so exercises – all, like Gerry's 2p exercise, were designed to coax some life back into my immovable hand.

She told me to try to move my fingers every single day. 'Even if you can't see your fingers moving,' she said, 'I want you to imagine them moving.' She told me that even if they weren't responding to my brain's instruction to move them, the neurons were firing. And that would speed up my rehabilitation.

Now that I had hope, I did exactly what Gerry Hughes and the OT recommended. I got busy every day trying to get my hand to move. It took time but within a fortnight, I was able to move my middle finger. It was a barely perceptible movement, but it was definitely there. With that – with the realization that this was working – I redoubled my efforts.

The next time I met the OT, she replaced my splint with a contraption with big steel springs on it, designed to give my wrist and fingers a proper workout. The kids on the school bus used to laugh at me and call me Edward Scissorhands, after the guy in the movie, but I didn't care.

I knew I was getting better.

Within six months, I could move my hand, my wrist, all of my fingers. The exercises had transformed it from a hunk of dead meat into a fully functional limb again.

The only problem was, no one would sign off on me going back to playing football.

My father brought me down to see a specialist in Belfast.

He told me, 'Other doctors are going to be telling you in twenty years' time that you shouldn't really be playing with that arm. But I think that you've developed the musculature around it so well, and your neural control is so strong, that you could give it a try.'

So my coach, Val Kane, let me go back playing, but he wouldn't let me into contact. Running, catching and kicking were fine, but no tackling.

I soon got sick of that.

I remember thinking, *this guy will never let me go into contact unless I show him I'm ready for it.* So one day, down on the school pitch, there was a tackling exercise that got really aggressive and physical. I jumped in, and I got through it.

After that, Val said, 'OK, you're ready to go.'

Within a year, I was on the Armagh minor team that won the Ulster title.

If I had listened to that surgeon, I would never have played another game of football and I'd still be going around cradling a useless arm. Because I had the good fortune to run into someone who did not accept the received wisdom – who saw the possibilities, rather than the tragedy – I am where I am.

It was an early and a valuable lesson.

When you hit a crisis, when your plan crumbles and your goals suddenly start to look impossible, that's when you need a growth mindset more than ever.

It also taught me the importance of anticipation. You can't just assume everything is going to go according to plan. You need to anticipate the obstacles that may get in your way, then imagine how you will overcome them.

YOU NEED TO ANTICIPATE THE OBSTACLES THAT MAY GET IN YOUR WAY.

Rehearse your reaction

I use 'scenario planning' with all of the elite athletes and business clients we work with. Scenario planning is all about working through the variety of contingencies which you will meet during any serious challenge.

It's vital to ensure that you're fully prepared, that you're blindsided by nothing.

With Ian McKeever, for example, we spent a lot of time working through the variety of pitfalls and potential disasters that threatened his goal of climbing the seven highest mountains in the world in world-record time.

→ *You're on Everest and you come across a dead body.* How will you handle it? (Many of those who die above 26,000 feet, in the mountain's 'Death Zone', cannot be recovered.)

→ *You're on K2 and you've got snow blindness.* What do you do?

→ *You've got frostbite, you can't feel your toes. It's so cold you can't even go to the toilet.* What will you do?

→ *You are experiencing intense loneliness.* How are you going to handle it?

→ *You have to leave Everest early.* How will you deal with it?

In your mental preparation, as you set off towards your mission, make sure you've factored in the 'something' that might go wrong. I'm not saying you should catastrophize about the countless horrible things that can happen, but do rehearse your reaction to setbacks.

What would you do if a major client disappeared in the morning – how would that impact your strategy?

What if you got made redundant?

What if you lost your funding?

Think about how you would react.

Yes, there might be a period of adjusting to the new reality – that's inevitable – but don't allow yourself to wallow.

Adopt a growth mindset. Picture how you're going to get back on your feet, think about what you would need to do to keep your mission on course.

Ask yourself where the opportunity lies – because adversity always generates opportunity.

6

STAYING THE DISTANCE

In the previous two chapters I talked about how to identify your mission and set up your goals to give yourself the best chance of success. Now I want to talk about maintaining the determination to deliver on those goals and explore strategies for getting things back on track if you start to lose sight of them.

Ditch the doubters

The first thing to say is that there will always be doubters. There are always going to be people who criticize, who are perhaps envious or resentful. You might call them 'dream stealers'.

I was at a nightclub at home. I was talking football with a Down supporter, and I told him that I believed Armagh would win an All-Ireland, and soon. This would have been around 1997, when we were ranked twenty-fifth in the country. The guy had just taken a mouthful of beer when I said this, and it was such an amazing joke that he spat out his beer, he was laughing so much.

I just repeated it. 'Armagh will win the All-Ireland.' Then I added, 'And I'll be on the team.'

In my local club, there were people who laughed when they heard I was on the Armagh squad. When I was selected for my first game, against Tyrone in the 1997 championship, the commentary from many would have been, 'Enda's not ready for this, he's not up to it . . .'

There were lots of doubts about my capability.

The week after we won the All-Ireland, in 2002, I was back in the nightclub at home. I met the guy who had spewed out beer when I told him, five years earlier, that we were going to do it. I just walked up and shook his hand. There was no need to say anything.

I learned not to care about what the wrong people said. If 10,000 people had told me, 'Enda, you're not good enough,' it just would not have mattered to me. I learned to ignore the people who knew nothing about being successful.

But the guys around me who knew what it took to be successful?

Those guys I listened to.

I became good at dissecting and classifying what was said to me. I listened carefully to the right voices. I took on board their advice, their opinions – I knew they could add value to my life.

And those who couldn't help me?

I filtered out what they said. I locked out their words. They were no use to me.

We now tell this to the athletes, professionals and artists we deal with: *Lock in what's important, lock out what's not.*

Perfect practice makes perfect

When I started working with the Leinster rugby team, one of my first assignments was with hooker Bernard Jackman. Twice a week, we worked on a mental training programme built around the line-out throws which form a central part of the hooker's role. We had this thing called a 'lollipop' – a long wooden pole with a hoop on the end – designed to give the hooker a target to aim for.

The training programme was comprised of sets of six throws each. The first set was just to get a feel for the ball, the second for routine, the third to get used to the target, and so on. We worked out a tightly choreographed set of moves, each of which was linked to a breathing pattern. The whole programme was built on repetition, with the aim of making the live line-outs on match days a matter of instinct.

We worked on these routines over and over again, until Bernard was sick of looking at me. We adapted the lollipop, drawing a smaller target on it to more finely tune the throws. And we also fitted it with a net, so I wasn't constantly running to retrieve the ball.

Hours and hours of the same routine.

Set stance . . . breathe . . . hold ball at chest . . . breathe . . . lift ball . . . breathe . . .

Throw.

Couldn't be simpler.

Nothing stopped Bernard Jackman from practising. Nothing.

The week before the Heineken Cup final, when Leinster was due to face Leicester Tigers at Murrayfield, he showed up at the practice ground dragging one leg after him, grimacing with every step. He couldn't walk. He looked exhausted.

'Bernard, what the hell's going on?'

'The knee's a disaster.'

He'd taken so many hits that year that his knee was inflamed. He told me he had to get up three times during the night to ice his leg for half an hour. And not only did he plan to show up to the final, but he also planned to play. Despite the injury, Bernard went through the exact same routine as he had in the previous weeks.

Over and over again.

Deliberate, focused practice.

He ended up playing most of that final. Leinster won, beating Leicester Tigers by three points in the end.

One thing I've learned through my years of working with elite athletes is that they all have one thing in common. It isn't that they're more talented. It's simply that they've put in more quality time, practising their skills. Watching world-class athletes practise is an education. They have an intense focus on what they are doing. It's as if there is nothing else happening in the world.

They are not the only ones. I remember the first time I saw *Riverdancer* Padraic Moyles practise. Talk about focus! Talk about detail! During that session, Padraic moved with the most intense combination of energy and concentration I had ever seen. It was as gruelling as it was graceful. I knew nothing about dance, of course. I couldn't say whether he was doing it right or not – it looked amazing, it looked perfect – but what bowled me over was the intensity of his practice. Utterly focused, utterly in the zone. If a bomb had gone off in the corner of the room, I'm not sure he would have noticed.

Sometimes, we'll pick up messages like this over our social media channels:

'I tried that resilience routine that you recommended, but it didn't work for me.'

'Gave that mental toughness ritual a try, but to be honest it didn't really make a difference.'

Here's the truth: *If you don't practise something over and over again, it won't stick.*

IF YOU DON'T PRACTISE SOMETHING OVER AND OVER AGAIN, IT WON'T STICK.

You will *not* get more resilient.

You will *not* get mentally tougher.

You will *not* improve your energy levels.

You will *not* get better at it.

Your mind is like your body. If you don't train your mind in the same repetitive manner – the same specific, focused, progressive manner – your mind will not change. Deciding that a particular ritual or programme doesn't work after one week, or two weeks, or a month is like deciding that lifting weights doesn't work after one week, or two weeks, or a month.

Practise.

It sounds so simple, it almost sounds stupid.

It's not.

Practise.

Keep on keeping on

I've set goals every year since I was fourteen years old. Back in my bedroom in my parents' house, my handwritten goals for 2001 are still pinned to the wardrobe. I planned to win the Ulster Championship, the All-Ireland, an All Star, the National League, and I also wanted to get a full-time job in professional sport.

By the end of 2002, the only thing Armagh hadn't won was the National League, and while I didn't have a full-time job in professional sport, I had a full-time job in amateur sport – I was coaching director with Ballyboden St Endas GAA club in Dublin.

I used to print off my goals on an old Mac we had at home and carry a copy around everywhere I went. I even had a laminated version I could take into the sauna and reflect on during recovery sessions.

I still bring my goals with me everywhere, and I look over them at least once a week, to the point where they're branded into my brain.

But there are days when sustaining that passion – no matter how great the meaning – is almost impossible.

No one is on fire all the time. Sometimes you drag yourself out of bed in the morning and nothing goes right, or you just feel flat.

The truth is that I've never met anyone who's passionate about what they do all the time. There will be struggles over the simplest things – it's just part of being human.

How to get back in the zone?

I have a series of rituals I use to try to spark the coals to life when they're smouldering. Try some of these.

Manage your mind

If your mind slips into that negative, pessimistic state, your emotions are going to follow suit. Mind management is all about flicking the switch. Turning off the negative, turning on the positive. All around you, there are things you cannot control. But there are always – always – things you *can* control.

You can't control the economy, you can't control the family, the company, the whole team, the whole community.

Flick the switch. Ask yourself, 'What is it I *can* control today?' What can you do that is entirely within your power, that comes back to a single decision and a will to stick with that decision?

For example, 'OK, I'm going to do one thing really well today – I'm going to eat well.'

Or, 'OK, I'm going to make sure I am thoroughly prepared for this one meeting.'

Or, 'Come hell or high water, I'm going to get in one hour of exercise today.'

Make a decision based on what you *can* control. Success at that mini-mission will make everything else seem that much more possible.

Have fun

When your fires are burning low and you just can't motivate yourself, go do something fun. Go spend time with friends, take a night off, go out and enjoy yourself. For me, it's getting in the kayak, or taking off on a mountain bike. No matter what's gone wrong, no matter how lousy I feel, within two hours I no longer care about what's happened, I'm back ready for anything.

About ten years ago, I got a call from Alan Matthews, who was then coaching the Longford Town soccer team.

'I want to win the FAI cup,' he told me. 'I've got a shoe-string budget, but I want to win the FAI cup.'

We started to meet up every two or three weeks to work out a plan. I didn't charge him anything; I wanted the experience of working with a great manager in a sport that was new to me. This was as much about my development as anything else.

It was a fascinating experience, during which I learned all kinds of things. For about three years, we met regularly and put together a plan which aimed to deliver the FAI cup. (And it eventually did, in both 2003 and 2004. I don't claim credit for that. The club's success was all down to the work Alan and the team had put in over successive years.)

Anyway, I'd often run our plan past my dad or my great friend and mentor, Dessie Ryan. Early on, Dessie pointed out something I was overlooking.

'This is all great, Enda,' he said, 'but how is the spirit in the camp?'

What I had missed out on was the element of fun. Nothing generates positive emotion in any group like having fun together. So we started to think about creative ways to generate a bit more craic in the squad. The week before the FAI cup final, we got them to stage mini-plays. One of the guys played someone who was totally convinced that Longford was going to win the next one. Little exercises like these were just brilliant for getting rid of tension and getting everyone feeling better about themselves and each other.

Think about the teacher who injected the most fun into the lessons at school, then about the class where you learned the most. Weren't they one and the same?

Every session we put together at McNulty Performance starts with fun. It relaxes you, it helps you to de-stress, and – critically – it helps you to learn.

Even the most serious work we do, at the highest corporate levels, involves an element of fun. We have just acquired a contract with Microsoft, which will involve running a series of high-performance team sessions in each of their regions around the world. Every one of those sessions will start with doing something fun. (It will, of course, be done organically. We won't be telling participants, 'Here comes the obligatory fun bit now!' There is nothing more guaranteed to put people off than being obliged to have fun.)

There is an interesting aside here, though – one that I hope you'll find valuable. Throughout the early part of my career with Armagh, I was a bit of a joker. I was as serious as hell on the pitch, but in the dressing room, on the bus, on team nights out, I took the piss out of everyone, I was up for a laugh. Then – I'll never forget it – one of the younger guys on the team did a newspaper interview, and he was asked, 'Who's the biggest joker in the squad.'

'Enda McNulty,' he said.

That was a wake-up call. I had put my whole life on the line for Armagh, I was one of the most professional players, I was one of the key leaders on the pitch – I thought so, anyway. I'd worked hard to be consistent, and yet here I was, in the paper, being identified as a joker?

The messing stopped overnight.

That great Irish rugby international Donncha O'Callaghan did the same thing. He made the decision to stop being known as the joker in the British and Irish Lions squad. He wanted one reputation – as a formidable professional. And that is exactly how he is thought of today.

Move

Run. Move. The reality is that motion changes your emotion.

Sometimes I find it difficult to get out of bed. Here's my trick if I don't feel like stirring. I've learned that by lying there and stretching, by starting to move my body very slowly while I'm still in bed, I wake it up and start to energize it. It makes it much, much easier to turn and climb out.

Try it. Once you get up, it's much easier to start to move your body more vigorously. And once you've started to move vigorously, you'll always feel better.

No matter how demotivated and stressed and anxious I am, I don't think I've ever started to move and not felt better – even when I was sick.

It's been well established that physical activity and exercise produce endorphins – some of which have been proven to have more powerful analgesic effects than morphine. Plus they're cheaper and easier to get hold of.

Movement is medicine.

Do it, you feel better.

It's that simple.

Have an adventure

By far the best way to energize yourself, to shake yourself out of a torpor, is to go do something *different*. Go have an adventure.

If I'm on my mountain bike in Armagh, heading up into the hills, and it's teeming with rain and there's little rivulets of rainwater running down the track against me, I'll look up and see a field, a small triangular field off in the distance, and I'll say, 'I've never been there before, I'll go explore that.' So I'll put the mountain bike on my back and run and climb and make my way, one way or another, up to that field.

I drive a lot of the people in our company crazy because I love to go off piste. I can't stick with the same routines and structures every day, I get bored. I don't like a structured, systemized culture. I try to create a dynamic, explorative, adventurous culture. I don't like maps (which, I guess, is part of the reason I get in trouble from time to time), I like to be able to explore, to wander.

You don't have to be out in the country to wander, not at all.

One time I was in New York. I'd done five days' training with a banking client and I was exhausted. I was heading back to the hotel and I had my gear with me, in case I had an opportunity to take a run in Central Park or somewhere. I had taken one of the many little alleyways down around Wall Street when, up ahead of me, this big black guy came out of a shabby little building to my left. I stopped and saw that it was a real, old-school, run-down, dingy boxing gym.

So I went over and pushed in through the door. It took a minute for my eyes to adjust; the place was dark but buzzing with activity. It was full of kids mostly, skipping, hitting the speedball, ducking around these ropes slung low across the ceiling. You could hear the squeak of gym shoes on the floor, the thud of gloves into heavy bags and the *patata, patata, patata* of the speedball. Old boxing bags hung from the ceiling, patched with white masking tape, there was saw-dust on the floor, graffiti all over the walls, and pipes criss-crossing the ceiling.

Bang in the centre of the place was the ring. The only area that was well lit. It was like an altar. There was a guy in there, dancing around. The coach had on a set of punch-mitts and the boxer was working on combinations of shots. All along the ring, there were kids, staring up at the two of them. Everyone was black.

A big guy came ambling over to me, 'What you want?'

Good question. What did I want? Then the idea struck me.

'I was wondering if there was any possibility I could do a session in here?'

'What? You?' It was as if it was the stupidest thing he'd ever heard. 'Get outta here, man.'

'I've got cash,' I said. 'I'm not looking for something for nothing.'

'Get lost.'

I scanned the dim interior of the gym and spotted an older guy. He was standing watching the guys in the ring, and he had the air of a man who was in charge.

'Hey!' I called out to him. 'I'd like to do a session in here. Hey!'

He turned and looked at me, then turned back to the ring.

'I can pay!' I called out to him. 'I just want a session in here.'

The first guy – the big guy – was about to shove me out the door. 'Why don't you just get the hell outta here, man?'

But then the boss started walking over.

'A session,' I said, 'an hour of coaching. No big deal. What do you say?'

He stared me up and down for half a minute before he spoke. 'You're crazy,' he said at last.

And I knew I was in.

The coach's name was Lenny. I couldn't tell what age he was – somewhere between thirty and fifty. He moved like a young man, but his voice was low and gravelly. And when he put his hand on your shoulder and stared hard at you, it was like he'd seen it all, several times.

The session was all about detail. Slowing things down. For the first fifteen minutes, we worked on nothing but stance. It was me and him in front of a mirror.

'Naw, man, your right foot's in the wrong position . . .
Naw, man, you gotta put your weight here, like this . . .'

Then he had me shadow-boxing in the mirror, going
through the most basic steps in minute detail, breaking
everything down, doing everything slowly and methodically.

For the first while, I was just itching to get to the next
stage, to get to the punchbag, to start hitting things.

But Lenny would lay a big hand on my shoulder. 'Naw,
man, you're not ready. Take it slow. Do it again. Get it right.'

When I started listening to him properly, when he saw that
I was paying attention, his attitude changed. He became
more engaged, less bemused by this weird white guy with the
strange accent. He saw I was serious, and he got serious.

After our session I watched him working with some of
the kids there. I've worked with a variety of household-name
coaches at the highest levels of professional sport, but I've
never seen anything like Lenny's attention to detail, the way
he broke complex moves down into their constituent parts,
the precision with which he instructed these kids. It was one
of the best coaching sessions I'd ever had, from this unknown
old guy in a run-down gym somewhere in Manhattan.

I walked out of there full of life, full of energy, absolutely
invigorated. I'd turned down that street two hours earlier,
weary and drained. Now I felt a different man.

Why?

Because I'd done something different – something different that also turned out to be something great.

If I'd just gone back to the hotel, if I'd gone for my run in
Central Park, I'd never have had that wonderful experience.

So go have an adventure.

MISSION – TAKE ACTION NOW!

1. *Start working on your goals.* Get a notepad, or use your laptop or tablet. Write down your goals, think about them, tinker with them. Is the meaning strong enough? Do you know what your mission is? Are your goals aligned with it? Is this something you really, really want?

2. *Stress-test your goals.* Are they SMARTER?

3. *Get an accountability partner.* Tell them what you plan to do and ask them to help you keep track of your progress towards your mission.

4. *Figure out what could go wrong.* Plan for it. Visualize how you would get back on track if something derails your progress towards your goals.

ENERGY

7

GET MOVING

No matter who you are, or what you do, energy is essential for your success. Energy is simply your capacity to do work. The more you have, the more you can achieve.

Whether it's in your personal or professional life.

Whether it's in sport or performance arts.

Whether you're an 18-year-old who wants to chase her dreams, or a 68-year-old who wants to learn to dance.

The good news is that, whereas time is finite, energy is renewable. While we can't create more time to do the things we want to do, we can make our time more fruitful by generating the energy to fill it with worthwhile, rewarding activities.

You develop more energy for all the roles and challenges you have in your life by making choices every day that enable you to replenish your supply.

Since having my first lesson in physical education studies from Val Kane, in the Abbey Grammar, the link between a healthy body and a healthy mind has fascinated me. For twenty-five years I have read, studied, practised, trained, meditated – all with a view to managing my energy.

I could summarize all I've learned like this.

➜ You need to eat exceptionally well.

➜ You need to get a good night's sleep and do so consistently.

➜ You need to move daily, and integrate exercise into your entire life.

➜ You need to build rest and recovery breaks into your day and week.

➜ You need to stay hydrated.

➜ You need to keep alcohol to a minimum.

➜ You need to minimize stress.

Exercise is so important that I'm devoting the rest of this chapter to it. (We will look at eating, sleeping and staying on track in the next chapter.)

You need more exercise than you think!

The conventional wisdom is that you need to get a half-hour of exercise into every day.

I disagree. You need one hour as a minimum.

Thirty minutes a day isn't going to change anything significantly. If you're trying to lose weight, if you want to boost your metabolism and energy levels, thirty minutes is not enough. If you want to flourish – if you want to get yourself into the best condition of your life, if you really want to tap into your potential and deliver on your commitments to yourself – you will need to get an hour of exercise every day.

My grandfather spent ten hours a day ploughing fields, lifting hay, churning butter, milking cows. He lived to be eighty-four years old, and was active and fit until a month before his death. Similarly, I have a good friend, Coli, who is a farmer in Armagh. He is in his late forties and is as healthy and as fit and strong as a twenty-year-old. Six days a week he starts his day at 5 a.m. and finishes at 6 p.m. His entire day is spent in motion, using all of his energy systems and muscle groups. No one can tell me that going to the gym for thirty minutes a day can compete with someone who is this active.

I know not everyone can exercise ten hours a day and/or work on a farm, but everyone has the choice to get moving. I have been hugely inspired by some of our clients who have been physically disabled and yet they still manage to exercise daily.

The American College of Sport and Exercise Medicine says that as a minimum requirement humans need to get thirty minutes of exercise, five times a week.

The UK National Health Service recommends *at least* 150 minutes of moderate aerobic activity every week *and* strength exercises that work all the major muscles on *two or more* days. Note the italicized words in that last sentence. *At least* 150 minutes. That breaks down into more than twenty minutes per day. Add in the recommended strength exercises and you're easily going to bring that up to thirty minutes. This, then, is the minimum.

I don't know about you, but I don't want merely to meet the minimum requirement.

HEALTH AND FITNESS SHOULD BE OUR FIRST PRIORITY WHEN WE WAKE EACH MORNING.

I want to thrive.

I believe in being proactive about health, and that health and fitness should be our first priority when we wake each morning. If we cannot make them a big priority then how can we grow a business, or nurture a family, or develop more meaningful relationships?

The idea of somehow managing to create an extra hour in the day to exercise may seem preposterous. Everyone is so busy. I don't know anyone who isn't. Our days are jam-packed with meetings and projects and childcare and laundry and shopping and driving . . . and a hundred and one other things.

Well, here's an even more preposterous idea. I said one hour *minimum*. On top of that, you also need to move regularly. Research that came out last year from my alma mater, Queen's University Belfast, found that sitting for long periods of time is just as dangerous for your health as smoking. It leads, among other things, to an increased risk of heart disease, obesity and diabetes. Think about it: human beings are not made to sit. We are not made to stare at a screen for ten hours a day. We have survived as a species because we could run, jump, climb, chase, swim, crawl, not lounge on the couch or sit hunched over a desk looking into a screen.

Dr David Raichlen in the School of Anthropology at the University of Arizona has done extensive research on our evolutionary history, primarily to see what it can tell us about improving human health and well-being today. His research has suggested that the transition to hunting and gathering thousands of years ago led to a biological need for physical activity simply to maintain health.

In other words, our bodies are designed for movement.

Mindset revisited

I'm looking for just one hour a day, not ten. If you've been up half the night with a sick child or one who refuses to sleep, if your job is so intense that it has spread out and taken over the rest of your life, the idea of carving out an hour to go for a run or a cycle or a walk just seems impossible. So let me tell you a story about someone who believed he couldn't possibly find the time to exercise, and what happened when he did.

Eamonn Sinnott is General Manager of Intel Ireland. To understand something about the industry in which Intel operates, you've got to know about Moore's Law. Moore's Law requires that computer processing power doubles every two years. Every two years, the processor has to be 100% more powerful than it was two years ago, or else half the size.

I can't think of any industry, or any sport, or any human endeavour that looks for that kind of return. It's like, if the Irish rugby team scores 500 points this season then it has to score 1,000 in two seasons' time, 2,000 in four seasons' time, and so on. But Intel does that. Every two years, it doubles the processing power of the chips it produces. That kind of thing doesn't happen by chance. It takes tremendous reserves of energy and ingenuity to soak up this relentless challenge and deliver, over and over and over again.

'We live in this volatile, uncertain, changeable and ambiguous world,' says Eamonn. 'Yes, it's fun, and dynamic, but it's competitive on a global scale, it's the nature of our industry.'

I started coaching Eamonn after he had been working in this dynamic, high-pressure environment for more than twenty-five years. Think about that – twenty-five years. I don't know too many athletes who have to perform, day in and day out, for twenty-five years.

Eamonn admitted that, while he had been on many excellent leadership courses and understood the importance of exercise and good nutrition, he found it difficult to work the principles he had learned into his day.

'There are so many things that make demands on my time. I can find it difficult to integrate everything.'

Long story short, to help him come up with a way of improving both his exercise and his nutrition, I agreed to spend some time learning about Eamonn's schedule and the particular challenges that he faced. And his schedule was as hectic as you would expect. He got up at 5.30 a.m. and typically had an eighteen-hour day filled with meetings, phone calls, emails, travel and the kinds of engagements that executives have to deal with the world over.

I pointed out that he didn't have to start running marathons or cycling hundreds of miles. Introducing movement into the day and hitting that daily minimum of taking 10,000 steps that so many fitness experts recommend isn't that difficult.

So Eamonn began to make simple changes to his routine. Instead of having meetings at a table in a room, he started conducting walking meetings. He began parking the car further away from the office.

'I was amazed,' he says, 'at how quickly you could cover ten thousand steps in a day. And also, how easy it was not to.'

The key to implementing these changes, as with implementing almost any change you can think of, brings us back once again to mindset. With a fixed mindset, exercise is one more thing that has to be squeezed into a day frantic with a thousand other things. With a growth mindset, it's the thing that makes all those other things more doable.

As Eamonn says:

'Maybe I used to think that it was selfish to focus on my own nutrition, exercise, recovery, but in working with Enda,

I realized it was selfish *not to*. Because when you don't get these things right, you're not as effective in work, you're not as present. You're not as clear in your thinking. You're not as available for all of the people that need your time. You're not available for your loved ones, the people closest to you. And I think that being at your best for the most important people in your life and the most important times in your day is a great way of thinking about how you manage your energy.'

It's not just aerobics

Because energy is renewable, you need to be renewing it constantly. Not just on the weekends, not just on holiday, not just when a gap opens up in your schedule. Energy management requires daily, if not hourly investment. To invest in it, as Eamonn Sinnott discovered, you don't have to run marathons. Your individual exercise needs are as individual as you are, and the range of things you can do is vast.

When most people think of exercise, they typically think about one type – cardiovascular. They think about running, or cycling, or walking, or going to the gym. But really you need to incorporate a range of exercise into your life, and do so consistently. In my experience, most people – even the elite athletes I've worked with – tend to spend all their time in the gym doing what they love doing. If that's strength training, they'll spend a disproportionate amount of time lifting, and neglect flexibility because it's not as cool. In order for exercise to deliver real results, however, it has to be balanced.

Incorporating yoga, Pilates, hiking or one hour of boxing into your week will give your body benefits that you will not get if you stick with running or some other cardiovascular exercise alone. If you can, you should get a personal trainer or proactive health expert to design you a programme around each of the following components of fitness.

Cardiovascular fitness
This is the body's ability to store and use energy.

Exercise modes that will develop this kind of fitness are those that get your heart pumping, for example, aerobic classes, spinning, High Intensity Interval Training (HIIT), running, cycling, hiking, Zumba, soccer.

Strength/resistance work
This is the ability of muscles to apply force.

Exercise modes that will develop strength are those that stress your muscle – for example, Olympic lifting, power lifting, calisthenics, bodyweight exercises, kettlebell routines, squats, free weights.

Strength training is great for losing weight, for keeping you strong and fit and for protecting bone and muscle mass. Studies vary in the details, but the research shows that you lose approximately 8% of your muscle mass every decade once you're over forty. Cardiovascular exercise won't hold on to that muscle for you, but strength training will.

Flexibility
This is the body's ability to maximize motion range at each joint. To develop flexibility you need to focus on stretching and mobility exercises.

Exercise modes that will help to develop flexibility include yoga, Pilates, Yogalates, body balance. Flexibility exercises are all about maintaining your body's correct alignment, the ideal posture.

Think about a car. If it's not balanced across all four wheels, you're going to wear out one tyre, or one part of one tyre, far more quickly than the others. So if you've got tight hips, or a tight ankle, or a tight lower back, activities like walking and running – even getting in and out of the car – will put undue pressure on different joints. Then, over time, you get wear and tear, aches and joint pain.

To maintain all the major joints and to keep yourself injury-free, you don't have to be a gymnast. But you do need to be flexible.

Office workers are particularly vulnerable to becoming stiff and immobile. If you sit in a chair all day, your knees will be close to your abdomen for long periods of time. When you stand up, the muscles in those areas will be resistant to lengthening. That's when you get pressure in your lower back, and this is why maintaining flexibility is so important.

Coordination

This is the ability to combine several separate movements in a single, unified movement.

Exercise modes that will develop greater coordination include boxing, t'ai chi, karate, salsa, or any field sport.

Agility

This is the ability to complete sets of movements as quickly as possible.

Tennis, badminton, squash and five-a-side soccer, for instance, are good ways of increasing your agility.

Balance

This is the body's capacity to control its centre of gravity in relation to its support base.

Exercise modes that will develop this include yoga and Pilates.

Rest and recovery

In any exercise programme, rest and recovery are vital. Disciplines like Pilates, t'ai chi, meditation and yoga help to relax the body and refocus you in the moment.

Combining an element of mind–body awareness into your programme does wonders for recovery and regeneration.

The other point to make here is that exercise, by its nature, has a strong mindfulness element. When you're exercising, you tend to be wholly focused on what you're doing, so you're less aware of your job, or your mortgage, or whatever it is that triggers stress for you.

Excusitis

It is so easy to find reasons to put off exercise for another day, or another week, or another month:

'I have three young kids, I never get enough sleep, I'm too tired to exercise.'

'I'm running a multi-million-dollar business, I don't have the time to exercise.'

'I've got a bad back, I can't actually exercise, the doctor says so.'

We hear things like this all the time from our clients. We listen, we sympathize, we understand the challenges. Then we get them to take out their diary and we go through it. Line by line, hour by hour, minute by minute, we figure out the gaps in the schedule, the one hour in every twenty-four that can be freed up for some sort of physical activity.

Get-out clause #1: medical advice

The standard advice before you start any programme of vigorous exercise is to go see your doctor first, and ensure you get a comprehensive health check before embarking on a significant increase in exercise. I strongly endorse that. But don't let it become a get-out clause.

'I'll read the book now, then I'll go see the doctor. And then, after all that, I'll start exercising.'

Move. Now.

You don't have to run five miles, just get up and walk, get up and stretch, go ride your bike.

Do it now.

MOVE. NOW. YOU DON'T HAVE TO RUN FIVE MILES, JUST GET UP AND WALK.

Find something positive to do today and every day, before you see your doctor. Then hopefully when you get the all-clear, make your plan and stick to it.

Get-out clause #2: genetics

Then there's the genetics excuse:

'My father was no good at sport, so I'm going to be no good at sport.'

'My mother was heavy, so I'm going to be heavy – what's the point in even trying to lose weight if my genes are against me?'

Eoin Lacey is a training and nutritional consultant who helps design fitness programmes for our clients in business, sport and performance arts. He has over twenty years' experience as a strength and conditioning coach – he is Conor McGregor's strength and conditioning coach – and he's given me a lot of help on this particular chapter.

He too is familiar with the genetics excuse. 'We've all inherited a deck of cards from our mother and father,' he says. 'These are our genes and we can't change them, but we can change the environment our genes are exposed to.'

He points out that a fixed mindset sees only the things that you can't change and decides that they trump everything else. A growth mindset sees the truth, which is that you are in control.

'Your whole body is constantly speaking to the environment, so when people say, "I'm fat because my mam was fat," I can understand why you would think that. But you're in direct control of what food you put in your mouth. Every time you eat something, every time you exercise, every time you don't exercise, you're speaking to those genes. You're either telling them to express themselves, or you're inhibiting them. People have a direct control over how their body is expressed.

'I weigh 100kg, my brother weighs 62kg. He has very similar genes to me, but he's a lecturer in the university. I'm a guy that works in a gym and tells people to lift weights. We have very different lifestyles, we exercise differently, we eat differently. I'm never going to be the best basketball player in the world because I'm not six foot six. But what I can do is I can train to be fit and strong and really express my genetic potential. I'm not going to let my genes restrict me. You've got to do the best with the genes that you have.'

Get-out clause #3: money

Not everyone is going to be able to afford a comprehensive fitness assessment or a fitness programme tailored to their exact needs. But if you can afford it at all, this is a great investment in your health, which will pay off instantly, and every day, in energy, in lust for life.

But if you don't have the money, don't let that be an excuse.

It costs nothing to go for a walk. You can use your body weight for strength training, and there are ample online resources to get a mobility and mind–body programme started. Here are some sites worth checking out:

→ dtsfitnesseducation.com/video
→ globalbodyweighttraining.com
→ stretchtowin.com
→ mobilitywod.com
→ teamexos.com

Get-out clause #4: body envy

Finally, don't be seduced by the images of perfectly sculpted bodies you see online. Even the ones that aren't Photoshopped may well be the product of steroids rather than exercise.

Being bulked up doesn't necessarily mean you're healthy. Overemphasizing strength training could leave you struggling for breath when you run for a bus. Lack of flexibility means you end up pulling a muscle the first time you try to do anything vigorous.

Sure, there are people out there who look amazing, who are in phenomenal shape, but that's their job – to train and prepare food. That's all they do. Your fitness goals need to be realistic. Aspiring to look like a fitness model or a celebrity is unrealistic.

Set your own goals. Focus on getting your body in the best shape for you.

Build it up

A good exercise regime must be gradual, it must allow you to integrate exercise into your life, and it must be progressive. Remember that exercising five times a week is much better for you than putting in one big session once a week.

As Eoin Lacey says:

'People watch videos of people exercising online and then they go to the gym, kill themselves and they're sore for a week afterwards. Don't do that. Start off on a walk, start off on a cycle, start off on a light fitness class with a friend – that gives you that great accountability element. Then build, increasing the time if you can, or the intensity, which allows you to get more work done in the same amount of time.'

Also, planning to do the one big session just dodges the necessity to find time in your diary every day. And you need that in order to make exercise habitual, to make it harder to stop once you start. Momentum is everything when you're trying to embed good behaviour and to make change stick.

Don't overdo it, especially in the early stages. That will only turn you off. Remember that rest and recovery are as important as cardiovascular activity or strength training.

Listen to your body. If day one is running, walking or cycling, and day two is squats and resistance training, then on day three do a restorative mind–body or flexibility session. Variety, in addition to delivering a balanced programme, also helps to keep you interested and engaged. It's easy to get bored doing the same things every day.

Keep your fingers on the pulse of how you feel – physically, mentally and emotionally. Some days I'm exhausted, and I know that it would be dangerous to go exercising, so I'll force myself not to. There are other days when I'm tired but I know that a good workout is what I need to invigorate me, so I go and work out.

Eoin's advice is the key to building up a sustainable exercise regime.

'The thing to avoid is yo-yo exercising – where someone goes hard at it for six weeks because they're going to a wedding, or there's a big AGM or something, and they want to look good in their suit, and then afterwards they just boomerang back to old habits. It's about doing something on a regular basis – we call it the MD basis. Your exercise has to be Maintainable and Doable.'

You need to be imaginative. You need to spot places in your week where you can insert movement and exercise.

Wrenching yourself away from your desk for a ten- or fifteen-minute walk, or stretch, or yoga session can be an awful struggle when you're staring down the barrel of a major deadline. But the truth is that taking a break delivers productivity improvements that more than justify it. You're not doing it despite the deadline, you're doing it in order to meet the deadline. There are plenty of studies out there demonstrating how integrating small elements of physical activity into your working day boosts productivity, engagement and concentration.

There are any amount of simple, everyday ways of making this happen. Here are some ideas.

→ Always take the stairs instead of the lift.
→ Get off the bus or train a stop or two early on your way to work so you can get in a brisk twenty-minute walk before you sit down for the morning.
→ Don't park at the door of the shop, find a spot that gives you a decent walk. Or cycle to the shops.
→ Don't get a trolley, carry a shopping basket instead.
→ Get down on your hands and knees to scrub the floor with a cloth, rather than using a mop.
→ Get out and clean the windows in your house, rather than have someone else clean them.
→ Link with a colleague and jog to work two days a week, or jog at lunchtime two days a week.
→ Arrange to have walking meetings with your manager rather than a meeting that is seated. You will be surprised at how much more productive it is.
→ Replace meeting-room meetings with walking to a cool coffee shop or an inspirational place, such as an old library.
→ Cycle to and from work three days a week.
→ Arrange to meet a co-worker or a friend in the gym three days a week.
→ Sign up for a fun fitness charity event every ninety days.
→ Sign up to a local gym and participate in a group fitness class three days a week.

Why not stretch yourself to experience one new type of exercise every two weeks?

Try Zumba, or Pilates, or boxing, or hiking, or kayaking, or surfing. All over the world there has been an explosion of new sports, such as snow-boarding and stand-up paddle boarding.

Why not try to experience a wide variety of exercises and sports so that you find out what you love? Aim to keep your body stimulated in different ways.

8

EATING, SLEEPING AND STAYING ON TRACK

Like most of our clients I am sure you have tried lots of diets, or had many phases whereby you changed your nutritional focus and choices. Maybe you have followed one of the most recent fads – say, cutting back on carbohydrates, or increasing your intake of fats. I am sure you have seen ads for miracle supplements that claim they will help you lose weight, or increase your energy, or perform better. You could fill a library with advice on nutrition – which I regard as the entrance ramp into good health.

My advice is to keep things simple, and to ensure you follow the most important rule of all regarding nutrition: eat real food.

Problems always begin when food is processed. The more ingredients on the box – the further it moves away from real to processed – the less healthy it is for you. The salt, the sugar, the processing – all of it takes food and turns it into something that isn't quite food any more.

Look at what has sustained the human race for thousands of years. Look at what our bodies have evolved to thrive on. There is an old phrase that we always repeat to clients in energy workshops around the world: 'If it doesn't swim in the sea, run on the ground, grow in the ground, or fall from a tree, don't eat it.' If you reflect on what you have eaten for the last week, or even the last day, how much of what you have eaten would fit into this category? And how much would not?

Everything you put in your mouth, or decide not to put in your mouth, affects your body, your health, your energy levels.

If you chose to eat nothing but a bowl of cereal for breakfast this morning, or just grabbed a cup of coffee and a scone on the way to work, you've made a choice about your energy levels for the rest of the day. You've decided to get by on not very much, you've decided that being wrecked by mid-afternoon is OK.

Ultimately, everything we eat impacts our energy, our body composition and eventually our health. If you want to maximize your energy, if you want to perform to the best of your ability, personally and professionally, if you want to live a long, healthy and vibrant life, eat real, lean, clean food 90% of the time. No more than 10% of the choices you make should be treats.

All of the elite performers we work with, without any exception, are hugely diligent in regard to what they eat and drink. They understand the impact that food has on energy, on cognitive performance, on their immune system, on their mood.

Intel's Eamonn Sinnott says:

'Information on nutrition changed my perspective completely. It's about realizing that food is there to fuel your performance, not to reward you. If you really want to perform in this wonderful industry of ours, you need to be at your best, so you need to fuel yourself in the best way possible.

'I tell the kids now, "We've got a diesel car. For a special treat, why don't we drive to the garage and give it some unleaded petrol today?" They laugh at that.'

And Eoin Lacey puts it like this:

'In the corporate world, decisions are made based on stats, details, profit margins and what makes business sense. The same should be true for your decision-making when it comes to food. Think of it as a business meeting. The only people there should be the people that are positively contributing to the meeting.'

THE REASON WHY MOST PEOPLE DON'T EAT WELL IS THAT THEY DON'T PLAN AHEAD.

The reason why most people don't eat well is that they don't plan ahead, and they are not educated to know what to eat, when to eat, how much to eat and how to eat. Rather than leave it to chance, why not spend sixty minutes at the weekend planning and preparing what you are going to eat for the week?

There are some fundamentals that will help you as you aim to significantly improve your nutrition.

1. *Remember the golden rule: eat real food.*
   If it is processed, if it has lots of ingredients, if it has loads of preservatives, if it has lots of packaging, you can be sure it will not have nearly the same nutritional value as real food.

2. *Eat small portions of food and eat often.*

This is almost counter-intuitive, I know. But if you want to control your appetite and regulate your blood sugar level to stay energized, if you want to be mentally alert, if you want to be lean and consistently have high energy, you must eat five or six small to medium snacks each day. If you eat every three hours, instead of having three big meals a day, you will control your blood sugar levels and your appetite, and you will also avoid mood swings and hunger pangs.

Frequent eating is like constantly throwing wood on to the fire. It cranks up your metabolism, and it burns more calories every time you eat. The opposite is also true; by not eating, often the fire smoulders and dies.

3. *Breakfast is your most important meal every day.*

The way we eat has shifted significantly in the last generation so that, nowadays, much of our food consumption happens late in the day. This is the Sumo Wrestling diet and it is the best way to gain weight and decrease performance. Eating late interferes with sleep, rest and recovery. Reverse the trend and try to keep your consumption between 6 a.m. and 6 p.m. A good breakfast is important in creating a solid nutritional base on which to build for the rest of the day.

Breakfast kick-starts your body and delivers an energy boost that you just can't get any other way. Research continually points to the benefits of eating a decent breakfast. I'm not talking here about eating an extra bowl of cereal out of a box. It is essential that your breakfast contains protein, carbohydrates, good fats and fibre. I'm talking about eating real food. A good breakfast boosts memory and concentration, and reduces the risks of heart disease, diabetes and obesity. Critically, studies have also shown that a good, healthy breakfast gives you the strength and endurance to engage in physical activity. Try it. Eat well first thing and watch how it impacts the rest of your day.

4. *Fats are fantastic.*

The anti-fat movement programmed us to believe that everything had to be low in fat. However, fats are essential for good health. All your cell membranes are made of fat. Fats release energy slowly and help you go from meal to meal without feeling that you are starving. Fats provide your body with some powerful nutrients and antioxidants.

Of course, not all fats are good. Many experts advise that saturated fats can raise cholesterol levels, clog your arteries and pose a threat to your heart. Cholesterol is a waxy substance that is in every cell in our bodies. But if we have it in excessive amounts it can cause blockages in our arteries and lead to strokes or heart attacks. Unsaturated fats don't raise cholesterol and perhaps can actually reduce blood cholesterol when substituted for saturated fats.

The best fats come from foods such as nuts, seeds and oily fish. Oils found in salmon, mackerel, lake trout, herring and sardines provide powerful fatty acids that have antioxidant properties and are essential for good cardiovascular health and mental clarity. A teaspoon of fish oil every morning and afternoon is a no-brainer.

5. *You need to drink enough water every day.*

We've known for a long time that dehydrated athletes get more injuries than their well-hydrated counterparts.

Staying hydrated is important for your energy levels. Proper hydration regulates your appetite. To ensure your body gets the water it needs, aim to increase your current intake by one glass per day until you hit ten glasses. Aim to drink two glasses of water in the morning when you wake. Take a two-litre bottle of water to work and sip throughout the day until it is all gone. Bring a bottle of water with you when you go to the gym and aim to sip water while you exercise.

Don't drink more than one glass at mealtimes, because it dilutes your digestive enzymes, and avoid drinking a lot of water prior to bedtime – getting up in the night-time to go to the bathroom interferes with your sleep. Adding a small pinch of Himalayan salt or Celtic sea salt to your water in the morning is great for absorption. And remember, if you're thirsty, you're already dehydrated.

Finally, integrate movement and hydration. Get into the habit of getting up from your desk every half-hour to go and get a drink of water.

6. *Change* how *you eat*.
Aim to be mindful as you eat. Slow down and be mindful of every bite and every chew. Challenge yourself to taste each forkful or chunk of food you eat. Put the fork down after each bite, and chew each mouthful of food at least ten times. Engage in conversation while enjoying your meal.

Everything you eat will either help or hinder your performance. Ask yourself before you put something in your mouth, *what will this do for me?*

So much of the process of building up and maintaining your reserves of energy is about establishing good habits and ditching bad ones. Eamonn Sinnott talks about how his thinking has shifted and how that has had a direct impact on his behaviour.

'Take a night out, a dinner out,' he says. 'Before I started this, I would think, "I'm going out tonight, I'd better not eat much all day today." Which meant that by the time I got out that night, I'd be overly hungry, which often led to overindulgence.'

That kind of thinking changes food from fuel into some kind of pay-off for a hard day. That's not what food is – it's not what it's ever been. Now, if Eamonn has a formal dinner in the evening, he prepares with a great breakfast and a good lunch. He can perform effectively throughout the day, and when evening comes he can still enjoy his food, eat well, get home at a reasonable hour and get a good night's sleep.

'There's no doubt that I personally feel a lot better,' he says. 'My thinking is a lot clearer. I'm more up for a challenge and know a lot more about how to control a busy day, a busy week, a busy month.'

On the menu

We can't be exhaustive here – and you'll find a huge variety of resources on healthy eating online – but Eoin Lacey has put together this range of meal suggestions, all of which are designed to fuel your body and give you the energy you need to make things happen:

You can use these templates as a jumping-off point to improve your eating habits.

They won't suit everyone. They emphasize protein, and have been drafted primarily with the carnivore in mind. There are, of course, great resources out there for healthy vegetarians.

Breakfast
Fist-sized portion of meat, good fats and carbohydrates in the form of vegetables.
- Salmon, eggs, avocado, salad
- Minute steak, green peppers, boiled eggs
- Turkey sausages, spinach, nut butter
- Chicken, onion and mushroom omelette

Lunch
Fist-sized portion of meat, 1–2 tablespoons of olive oil or butter, vegetables and a small portion (25g) of complex carbohydrates (sweet potato, rice, quinoa).
- Prawns, avocado, mixed leaf salad
- Chicken, red peppers, quinoa, rocket and watercress salad
- Lamb mince with herbs/spices and lettuce in a wrap
- Chicken and vegetable soup
- Seafood chowder

Dinner
Fist-sized portion of meat, a large portion of above-ground vegetables, together with sweet potatoes, rice, quinoa, etc.
- Fillet steak, asparagus and sweet potato
- Darn of salmon, broccoli and brown rice
- Chicken stir fry, peppers, onions and quinoa
- Spaghetti Bolognese and courgette pasta

Sleep is the secret pill

Over the course of two basketball seasons in 2010, Cheri Mah, a researcher in the Stanford Sleep Disorders Clinic, conducted a research project into the value of extending sleeping hours for elite basketball players.

The researchers asked the players to keep their normal sleep schedule (sleeping for six to nine hours) for two to four weeks, then aim to spend ten hours in bed each night for the next five to seven weeks. During the study period, players stayed off caffeinated drinks and alcohol. If travel prevented them from getting ten hours' sleep, they agreed to take day-time naps to make it up.

At the end of the sleep extension period, the players ran 282-foot sprints in a faster time (16.2 seconds versus 15.5 seconds) than they had before the experiment. Shooting accuracy during practice also improved, fatigue levels decreased, and athletes reported improved performance in practices and games.

Sleep isn't just good for basketball players. Recent research on the organizational cost of insufficient sleep, carried out by the management consultancy firm McKinsey, reported on a range of studies showing that sleep was beneficial for a host of cognitive functions: insight, pattern recognition, and the ability to come up with innovative and creative ideas.

Obviously, few of us are going to be able to find the additional time to get ten hours' sleep at night. But the lesson here is that getting enough good-quality sleep is essential if you are going to perform at your best. Intel's Eamonn Sinnott understands the ease with which you can fall into bad sleep habits.

'It's very easy when the house quietens down and the kids are in bed to slip away to your laptop and start doing emails. A couple of hours can go by without you even knowing it. All of a sudden, it's midnight and you've lost that precious couple of hours' sleep before twelve where you can really recover.'

As with exercise, improving your sleep is about trying to establish good behaviour. In your transition from waking to sleeping, you need to begin your wind-down an hour before bedtime. Try to establish rituals that ensure you

IMPROVING YOUR SLEEP IS ABOUT TRYING TO ESTABLISH GOOD BEHAVIOUR.

have a great transition from waking to sleeping.

Turn off all the screens one hour before bed, and put your phone on flight mode. Get yourself into easy, comfortable clothes, ready for bed. Dim the lights in your sitting room and bedroom, then put on some chilled-out music. Do some very gentle stretches while you focus on slowing down your breathing.

A great – and proven – ritual just before you go to sleep, helping you to build your resilience and improve your emotional well-being, is Martin Seligman's 'What's Working Well' exercise. Take ten minutes as you lie in bed to remind yourself of three things in your life that are working well.

These things can be small:

'I had coffee with a friend.'

'I contributed well to a meeting at work.'

Or they can be huge:

'I have two healthy children.'

'My husband is a great support in my life.'

After each item, say *why* it happened. Name the reason. And if you wake in the middle of the night, focus on these good things in order to drive away the worries that tend to creep into your mind in the small hours. A range of studies have shown that this simple little exercise markedly increases happiness and decreases depression.

Here are some more tips for good sleep hygiene.

→ Your bedroom should be like the bat cave, completely dark – put in black-out blinds if your window dressing is too thin to block out light.
→ Spend ten minutes or so gently stretching as you focus on your breathing.
→ Have no mobiles or iPads or computers in the bedroom.
→ Get an alarm clock, instead of using the alarm on your mobile phone.
→ Do not have a TV in the bedroom.
→ Bedrooms should be neither hot nor cold, but cool.
→ So that your feet aren't wedged tight, do not tuck your bedcovers in under the mattress.
→ Make sure you've got comfortable sleepwear, sheets, pillows and covers.
→ Try to get an extra hour of sleep once a week – preferably on a Sunday.

Morning rituals

I'm a huge believer in the value of starting your day well, in taking the time to establish a series of energy-boosting rituals to set you up for the challenges ahead. Again, these take time, but I'm sure that taking that time has done wonders for my energy levels and my appetite for life.

The days when I perform to my potential and the days when I feel I make the most positive impact are the days when I get my '90 minute peak performance kick start' done. It goes as follows.

→ Get up and put on a comfortable pair of long, warm shorts and a warm, cotton T-shirt.

→ Go into the sitting room and roll out a yoga mat on the floor.

→ Light a small candle.

→ Open the curtains.

→ Put on relaxing, meditative music.

→ Sit on the yoga mat in the cross-legged (lotus) yoga pose.

→ Meditate for ten minutes.

→ Then do gentle yoga stretches for fifteen minutes, remaining conscious of breathing in and out through the nose.

→ Spend ten minutes writing a list of all the things you are thankful for in your life.

→ Do activation exercises – press-ups, squats, plank, bridge, sit-ups – for fifteen minutes, all executed while repeating affirmations (see below).

→ Meditate for a further ten minutes.

→ Shower.

→ Dress.

→ Prepare healthy breakfast.

→ Set goals for the day.

→ Plan the day.

By 'affirmations' I mean a series of short, positive, present-tense statements that boost confidence and self-esteem.

I strongly recommend that you create your own affirmations. And that you continually use them.

Here are some of those I use, and some of the best that I have encountered along the way:

'Every day, in every way, I get stronger and stronger. More balanced. More connected with my mission. Happier.'

'As my self-confidence, my self-esteem, my self-belief are so strong, I ooze confidence in all scenarios.'

'I continually play to my strengths, and I back myself in all scenarios.'

'I am confident, articulate, humble, passionate and caring when communicating to people.'

'Setbacks, defeat and failure are merely an opportunity for me to grow and become stronger.'

'I am extremely thankful for all the good luck and fortune I have had in my life.'

'Whatever happens to me, I will handle it.'

'This too shall pass . . .'

'I am strong, I am confident, I am resilient, I am calm, I am in control of my emotions.'

Pick one or two, or even better, craft your own. Learn them. Repeat them, over and over again, almost like prayers.

You'll be amazed how powerful they can become.

And you'll be amazed by how you will use them at the times when you feel low or fragile.

Preparing for a fall

No matter how much you work on it, inevitably you will encounter problems along the way. In the previous section, I talked about the need to plan for setbacks when you set out to accomplish your mission. It's just the same when it comes to energy management.

Expect to stumble. Plan for it.

Expect the day you get the flu and can't exercise.

Expect the injury that puts a stop to all of the good habits you've developed.

Expect the crisis that throws your plan into disarray.

Expect it. Because it's going to happen. That's just the way it is.

Bad things happen all the time, and they will happen to you.

In the 2003 National League quarter-final against Laois in Croke Park, I went for a ball on the ground, and as I did, an opposing player dropped on my shoulder and my shoulder popped out. It was the most painful thing I'd ever experienced – so bad that I passed out and woke up in the dressing room, surrounded by medics.

In the hospital, a few days later, the doctor told me that I'd be lucky to be back playing football within three months.

This would have been a crushing blow, if I had accepted what the doctor said.

I didn't.

The experience of breaking my arm nine years earlier had proved to me that you do not have to accept the conventional wisdom. You do not have to accept the most pessimistic prognosis. You do not mope around, bemoaning the terrible thing that's happened, nor do you obsess about the disaster.

You find a way out of it.

In the years since I broke my arm, I had learned the difference between a growth and a fixed mindset. Within hours of dislocating my shoulder, I was thinking about the muscle mass around it, and the fact that I was going to lose it if I had to keep my shoulder still – which, of course, was what the doctor had told me to do in order to allow the joint to repair itself. But if I lost that muscle mass, he was right: there would be no way I'd be playing football at the highest level for years.

So that night, I started moving it. Not much, just enough to keep the muscle stimulated. I had a great physio, Alan Kelly, who I had been going to for years. Within three days of the dislocation, he had my arm out of the sling and was showing me how I could move it safely. Within a week, I was doing light dumb-bell bicep curls.

I was back playing for Armagh in time for the All-Ireland quarter-final a few months later, and I stayed playing at that level for the next seven years.

As a footballer you're always aware of injury. You always know that a bad tackle, or a mistimed jump, or a little bit of bad luck can put you out of action. I hadn't obsessed about the possibility of injury, but I had worked out how I would deal with it if it came. I used this time to get fitter, to get leaner, to work on my skills, to rest better, to improve my mental preparation.

So when the big injury came, I was ready.

Once again, it comes back to a decision, *your* decision.

Everything depends on how you respond when things start going against you. That's what we're going to talk about in the next section. Resilience – what it is, and how you get it.

ENERGY – TAKE ACTION NOW!

1. *Go out and buy a new journal.* Inscribe it with your name and the date, and call it 'My energy, health and fitness journal'. Write out three or four goals for yourself that you will focus on in regard to energy and health and fitness for the next ninety days.

2. *Write out a plan for the next week.* Work out how you are going to build in sixty minutes of exercise each day.

3. *Book a comprehensive health check.* Make the call now.

4. *Exercise today.* It does not have to be massively intensive. But take action today and go for a sixty-minute brisk walk, or go for a jog, or take the bike out of the garage and go for a sixty-minute cycle. If the weather is too bad, get down on the floor and do sixty minutes of body-weight circuits. Move. You will not regret it.

5. *Call a personal trainer or a fitness consultant.* Arrange a one-to-one session. Ask them to write a comprehensive fitness plan for you.

6. *Arrange to meet a nutritionist.* Get them to analyse your nutrition over the last month and to write a plan for the next ninety days. Check in with them every week.

7. *Talk with your family about how you will all become healthier and fitter.* Have fun with the conversation, but try to inspire them to eat more healthily, to move more and to become aware of the choices they make every day.

8. *Plan a family workout over the next week.* Schedule a walk, a game of golf, a cycle, a hike or a swim. Be creative. Generate a little healthy competition; see who can walk with the best posture, or who can hike to the top of a hill the fastest.

RESILIENCE

9

BOUNCING BACK

The bomb went off at half past eight. I was brushing my teeth in the bathroom when I heard the explosion. I was nine years old, and it was the loudest sound I had ever heard.

Straight after the explosion came the pause. Silence. For a second, the world held its breath. Nothing moved.

The stairs, I thought, *the stairs is after collapsing*.

Next came the sound of shattering glass, and all of the windows in our house rattled. My sister, who had been outside, ran in, screaming. All of us kids went into panic mode.

But my mother did not.

Even clearer than my memory of the blast, or the windows, or the screams is how composed she was. How calm she was. We were shocked and shaken and fragile, but she was centred and ice-cool.

I remember how she dealt with us. There was no fuss, no fluster. She calmed us down, then quietly went to see what had happened. Once she was sure it was safe, it was business as usual.

'Get your gear bag,' she said to me, 'you've got training today. There's no day off, get on your bike.'

As we went off to school, we could see the smoke and soot rising from among the trees just a few hundred metres from the house. Later, we would learn that it was an IRA car bomb, and that three people had died in the blast.

There is a story told about Nelson Mandela by Richard Stengel, the guy who collaborated with him on his autobiography *Long Walk to Freedom*. They were on a flight in a six-prop plane in Natal when Mandela nudged Stengel and pointed out the window. One of the propellers wasn't turning.

'Richard,' said Mandela, 'you might want to inform the pilot that the propeller isn't working.'

Stengel got up, went to the cockpit and told the pilot, who of course knew all about it. He had already radioed ahead, and told Stengel that the emergency services were waiting in the airport with a fleet of ambulances. Stengel, utterly terrified, came back and reported this to Mandela.

Mandela listened and nodded solemnly. 'Yes,' he said, and then calmly picked up his newspaper and resumed reading.

Though panic broke out initially, Mandela's relaxed demeanour had a calming influence on everyone else.

The plane landed successfully, and later, when Mandela and Stengel were alone together, the great man turned to the writer and said, 'Man, was I scared up there.'

Mandela was well aware of how those around him regarded him. Because of who he was, he couldn't show fear. And by not showing fear, he made those around him less fearful.

When I heard this story, years later, I was reminded of my mother that morning in Armagh.

Was she fearful? Was she nervous?

Of course she was.

But because she was calm, so were we. It was the best example of being cool under pressure that I have ever seen in my life.

What Mandela and my mother both showed in sudden and frightening situations were impressive levels of strength and composure. Their self-possession came out of enormous reserves of resilience that stood to them in the moment of crisis. Resilience is definitely one of my mother's greatest qualities. She has been a life-long inspiration to me, as she is to the thousands of kids she taught and the wide array of people in the community that she works with. Resilience like hers is contagious.

Resilience is simply the ability to bounce back from adversity.

And resilience is vital. Because no matter who you are or what you do, you're going to meet adversity. It is definitely coming in one form or another. Something is going to hit you out of the blue on a Tuesday afternoon, right when you are least expecting it.

RESILIENCE IS SIMPLY THE ABILITY TO BOUNCE BACK FROM ADVERSITY.

You get dropped from your team, or the team loses unexpectedly. Maybe your cruciate ligament ruptures and it starts to look like you'll never play again.

You lose a big contract in business, or you are told that you will be made redundant by the end of the year.

Your right-hand man resigns, taking half your team with him. Maybe sterling drops through the floor and your export earnings disappear.

Your partner turns to you one morning and tells you it's over. He doesn't love you any more, and he wants to leave your home.

You discover one of the kids is getting bullied in school. Or is the bully.

Your teenage son is worried about his gender identity.

Your mother has been diagnosed with early onset dementia.

To use the analogy of a boxer, when we get hit our reserves of resilience will determine how we respond. Inevitably, we're all going to go to the floor. But do we stay down for ten seconds and then get up, find our bearings and fight back?

Or are we knocked out completely?

The building blocks of resilience

Some of us are born with naturally high levels of resilience, and some without very much at all.

But here's the good news: *if you're fragile, if you're cracking under pressure, you don't have to accept it.*

Though it is hard work – and takes consistent, focused effort – you can develop your resilience in the same way that you can develop your physical fitness.

So how do you go about becoming more resilient?

Back in 2008, the US army approached the father of positive psychology, Martin Seligman, and asked him exactly that question. The army had been mired in a succession of wars for more than two decades at that stage, and its veterans were suffering high rates of Post-Traumatic Stress Disorder (PTSD), homelessness, addiction, divorce and suicide.

In his book *Flourish*, Seligman, who's been a great inspiration to me, and whose work I've been following for years, recalls his lunchtime meeting at the Pentagon with George Casey, the US army's Chief of Staff. Casey told him that he wanted to create an army that was as fit psychologically as it was physically. He asked Seligman to design a programme that would create an armed force as resilient as any in the world.

Nearly thirty years of research had already shown Seligman that resilience can be taught, and that depression and anxiety can be reduced, through what he called 'Resilience Training'.

He told George Casey something unexpected – that while the army might have seen thousands of soldiers struggle with depression and PTSD, there were others who would actually have experienced post-traumatic *growth*. In other words, while some people initially spiral into helplessness and despair in response to a traumatic episode, within a year they will be better off than they were before the trauma occurred.

As Seligman points out, these are the people Nietzsche was talking about when he said, 'That which does not kill us makes us stronger.'

The $145 million programme that followed was designed to teach resilience skills to the entire army. I have had the opportunity to collaborate with one of the tutors on this resilience programme. Her job was to train the trainers in the US army – the sergeants and staff sergeants whose job it was to lead men and women in battle. The amount of science and research Seligman and his team applied to this pro-gramme is extremely impressive. And yet, it is very practical, based around Seligman's tried and tested model – PERMA.

Put simply, well-being can be broken down into five key elements – Positive emotion, Engagement, Relationships, Meaning and Accomplishment. PERMA.

By working on each one of these elements in turn, it's possible to reinvent your psychology and create a more resilient version of yourself. For the rest of this chapter we will look at each element of PERMA in turn.

Positive emotion

Between stimulus and response, there is a choice.

The stimulus is getting sacked, getting sick, getting dumped, getting dropped. The stimulus is somebody else's choice, it's outside of my control.

But the response? The response is my choice.

When I was setting up the company in 2005, the banks were not particularly supportive. All I heard when I went looking for finance was 'No'. At the time, I was working out of a bedroom in Ranelagh, and often had to rely on my brother Paul to pay my rent. Without his support during those first few years, there's no way I could have got the business off the ground. I used to meet clients in a local café. If I needed to use the internet or do any photocopying, I had to go round the corner to an internet café that doubled as a launderette. (Once I was on the phone to a prospective client when a woman came in shouting about a load of whites that had turned orange in one of the machines.)

I got a meeting with two business advisers in a big Dublin consultancy. These guys, I hoped, would give me the backing I needed. I met them in a beautiful fifth-floor office, all glass and chrome, with amazing views over the city. Both wore immaculate, tailored suits and had perfect hair. They weren't much older than me. I told them what I wanted to do – set up a business to help people and teams achieve their potential.

I knew almost immediately that this wasn't going to work. Both were sitting back in the upholstered leather chairs. Their body language screamed lack of interest. There was a lot of looking out the window, shifting around and watch-checking. I was only halfway through my presentation when one of them sat forward and interrupted me.

'There's no future in what you're talking about, none at all. There is no market for what you do. And, anyway, what can business learn from sport? We would recommend that you go and become a coach again. Stick to what you know, stick to the knitting.'

I left, disgusted, and stormed off down the street.

Once I'd walked off my anger, I went into a little café and ordered a coffee. As I sat there thinking about what had happened, I made a decision. I decided that I wouldn't let this negative experience stop me. Not only would it not stop me, but I'd use it to help me. I'd take all that scepticism and complacency and dismissiveness and I'd turn it into fuel.

In other words, I chose to turn all that negative emotion into positive emotion.

I said to myself that if I ever found myself on the other side of the desk, if I was ever in their shoes, I would not behave so ungraciously. I'd treat whoever it was with respect, I'd try to lead them, even if that meant advising them against whatever it was they had planned. I would try to be encouraging, and if I had doubts about the viability of a project I would be as constructive as possible in my feedback.

I decided that when I met young business people or young athletes, I'd tell them, 'When you meet failure, when you meet rejection, when you meet cynicism, turn it into fuel for the fire.'

So I didn't go back to the knitting. I kept forging ahead. I made a commitment there and then that I would work day and night to make my business work. Some day, I said to myself, that company would be asking *me* for help.

And that's exactly what happened. Six years after that meeting, I was back in the same office giving them advice about their organizational mindset.

When people are resilient, they condition themselves to insert positivity between stimulus and response. They understand that they have a choice in how they respond to the stimulus.

Choice is critical to building resilience and learning how to bounce back. We can work on our psychological make-up and figure out strategies for managing our emotions. We can give ourselves the space to be in charge of our reactions. And we can choose to react positively.

YOU CAN CONTROL YOUR PSYCHOLOGY.

Become aware of that simple fact. You can control your psychology.

This was one of the fundamental tenets of Viktor Frankl's wonderful book, *Man's Search for Meaning*. Frankl survived the Nazi death camps. In the midst of the horror of that experience he discovered a liberating truth.

> Everything can be taken from a man but one thing: the last of the human freedoms – to choose one's attitude in any given set of circumstances, to choose one's own way.

No matter how he suffered – and Frankl and his comrades suffered terribly – the camp guards could not have any say over how he reacted to the worst that they could throw at him. He still had a choice to make.

It's the same for all of us.

When you suffer a setback, recognize this: *I am in control of how I respond.*

You control your psychology here. Not the perpetrator, not the person who sacked you, not the person who dropped you, not your disease. You choose how to react.

That's the first step. You use that control to steer yourself away from the black hole. To replace the negative emotion with a positive emotion.

There is a range of things you can do to help you focus on growth and opportunity. I'll talk about them in the next chapter, 'Resilience in action'.

One other thing that I've always found helpful is putting failure into context.

I always took defeat hard. When Armagh lost the All-Ireland final to Tyrone in 2003, I could feel myself beginning to sink into the usual deep depression that tended to consume me after big losses. But the day after the All-Ireland, a young guy from my parish took his own life. The first thing I had to do when I got back home was go to his wake.

That was a wake-up call. Yes, it was bad that Armagh got beaten in the All-Ireland, but here I was shaking hands with the parents of a young kid who were devastated because their son was dead.

Reality bites: 'Yes, it was a big defeat. But it's just football. *Get over it.*'

Engagement

Engagement is all about doing stuff that you love. When you're totally absorbed in something – like golf, or bridge, or whatever it is – you're no longer mired in crisis. You're free from it.

When you've suffered adversity, more than anything else you need positive engagement with something you enjoy doing. It's all about trying to get yourself into what's known as the 'flow' state – that's when you're so absorbed in what you're doing that the time just flies by without you noticing. I'm going to talk about flow in more detail in Chapters 15 and 16.

I had a guy in the office a couple of weeks ago who's been through two tough years. Everything that could go wrong went wrong. He got cancer, his wife got cancer, and they're in all sorts of financial difficulty. He talked about a perform-ance arts project that he was passionate about. When he did, his demeanour changed entirely. Discussing it made his eyes light up. He told me he was going to have to give it up, because he was too tired to keep it in his life. I told him not to, if at all possible.

If you really want to build resilience, you need to keep doing the things you love.

Relationships
The research is very clear. The more positive relationships we have around us, the more resilient we're going to be.

IF YOU'RE SUFFERING THROUGH SOMETHING, DON'T WITHDRAW.

If you're suffering through something, don't withdraw. It will only make you more fragile.

Think of people who are down and out. They don't have anybody at all. The most resilient people I meet always have a very strong support structure. You need to maintain strong relationships in all areas of your life – with your partner, your children, your family, your friends and colleagues, your community.

We know that if a soldier returns from active service with a very strong support structure around him, he's much more likely to be resilient and experience post-traumatic growth.

Without positive relationships around you, you become brittle.

When the Armagh team suffered a big defeat, we were good at getting together in little huddles, asking each other, 'What do we need to improve here, guys?' and talking each other back to positivity.

I remember my teammate Cathal O'Rourke calling at the house on the Tuesday after Kerry had beaten us after a replay in the 2000 All-Ireland semi-final. We were in the backyard, kicking a ball around.

Cathal said, 'We have to build on this. It wasn't good enough this time – how can we beat this Kerry team?'

Just two days after the biggest defeat of our sporting lives, Cathal was already looking forward, trying to find a way to turn that defeat into victory (which we did, two years later, when we beat the same Kerry team in the All-Ireland final).

Google recently released a study of the things that characterize its most successful teams. The study looked at the five 'key dynamics' always found in the company's best teams. Far and away the most important of these dynamics is psychological safety: 'Do I have the freedom to take risks without fear of ridicule?' Obviously, this would be impossible without good relationships on the team, without high levels of trust.

No matter what kind of team you're talking about – whether it's an IT team, or an international rugby side, or a local drama group – the tighter the relationships, the more resilient the group.

And the more resilient the individual members of the group.

Meaning
I've talked about this before. Meaning is crucial:

'Why am I putting in an eighty-hour week this week?'

'Why am I going to spend nearly ten years studying to be a doctor?'

'Why am I going to work on this relationship?'

'Why am I getting up at five in the morning to train for two hours?'

Nietzsche said: 'He who has a *why* to live for can bear almost any *how*.'

Humans will endure anything if we have a big enough reason. We will climb any mountain. No matter what the adversity, if the motivation is strong enough, we will find a way.

One thing I have found repeatedly is that the more successful the person, in any walk of life, the stronger and more developed their sense of purpose. They're not worried about failing here, or failing there, or facing any kind of adversity. Their sole concern is that they get there. And that purpose could be anything – from providing a decent life for their children, to building a global company, to making it on to an international rugby team.

Look at Father Peter McVerry. His motivational stamina is off the scale. He's been fighting for the rights of vulnerable young people in Dublin for the past forty years, trying to get them homes, trying to give them normal lives, advocating for their interests in debates about our society and economy, asking some very challenging questions. He's not about to stop, despite the seemingly insurmountable obstacles he faces. He's going to keep going.

If the meaning is strong enough, you'll find your way around any obstacle.

Say you've been defeated in business, or defeated at sport, or defeated in life. If there's no compelling reason to keep going, well, why wouldn't you just stop? Why would you not pull back and do something else?

IF THE MEANING IS STRONG ENOUGH, YOU'LL FIND YOUR WAY AROUND ANY OBSTACLE.

I didn't win any All-Irelands for the last three years of my career. All-Irelands? I played zero minutes for the last three years of my inter-county career with Armagh – nothing in either the league or championship. I doubt there's a single footballer or hurler in the history of either game who has got zero minutes of play over that kind of time frame.

Though I wasn't getting picked, I still used to warm up six or seven times during a game. I'd climb up out of the dugout and go through my routine on the sideline. I knew I was in the best shape of my life and I used to think that by running past the coach, showing the crowd the shape I was in, someone would say, 'Maybe it's time to put Enda in.'

One day we were playing Cork in a league match. I wasn't picked, of course. I was out warming up, going through my usual routine, when I heard a voice I knew well calling me from the crowd, 'Enda! Enda! What are you at?'

It was Tony McEntee, the man who, years earlier, had stood up in the hotel in Newry and declared that it would be a disgrace if we didn't win an All-Ireland. We had won our

All-Ireland at that stage and, one by one, the members of that team had taken the high road and retired.

All except me.

'Enda, you're making a joke of yourself. You should be out here with me. It's over.'

There it was, the man who had ignited that ambition for All-Ireland glory, signalling the time to stop. I just smiled at him and went back to my warm-up.

I never left that team, I never quit.

The following year, I wasn't selected for the panel. No one called me, no one phoned me up to say, 'Thanks, Enda, but you're out'. I was in the States when a journalist rang to know what it was like to get dropped after so many years.

Now – was that failure?

The thing is that I always loved training. When the kit man, Paddy McNamee, would be closing the pitch in Armagh and turning off the lights, I'd still be out there, practising my kicking.

'Enda, for God's sake, I'm going home.'

'Paddy, I need to practise my skills, I'll be done in a minute.'

So why did I keep coming back?

Well, I thought I still had a huge amount to offer.

I was training brilliantly. I believe I trained better in those three years than ever before. By then I was working with the Leinster rugby squad, as well as many professional athletes, and was learning a more comprehensive approach to all aspects of preparation. I was doing Pilates and yoga. I was doing speed development. I was getting physical therapy. In short, I was massively engaged in getting better. And I loved it. So even though the selectors weren't picking me, I was loving the training.

Also, I knew I had massive capability as a leader: I had the mental toughness and the experience. Deep down I still believed that eventually somebody would say, 'Actually, Enda, I was wrong. You're the man for the job.'

I kept doing it too because I wanted to prove that I could. Everybody said that I couldn't. And ultimately I kept doing it because I wanted to be a footballer. That's what I'd always dreamed of, and you don't give up a dream like that too easily.

Not getting picked was a bitter pill to swallow. Certainly, at the beginning, I felt extremely hard done by. But when I could detach myself and look at the situation clinically, I knew that what I was going through was giving me a much richer range of experiences than those based on success and nothing else.

People don't come to us when they're on top of their game, when they're rocking and in the zone week after week. They come after they've been dropped, or when they find themselves in a performance slump. I had been playing football at the highest level, but now I was on the bench. This gave me a much greater ability to empathize, to identify with elite athletes who weren't being given the chance to prove themselves.

I found out more about myself in those last three game-less years on the Armagh squad than I did in the previous eleven years when I was almost ever-present. In fact, I would say that they were the most successful years of my inter-county career. That may sound crazy, but everything depends on how you measure success.

I don't think of success in terms of medals, or inter-national caps, or the size of my bank balance or house, or the number of followers someone has on Twitter. I like how the legendary American basketball coach, John Wooden, viewed success. He was successful by any measure, a house-hold name in the USA and one of the most decorated coaches in the history of any sport, let alone basketball. His teams clocked up an unprecedented seven successive national college championships, as well as countless other honours. Wooden was a legend right up until his death at the age of ninety-nine, in 2010.

I learned his definition of success by heart years ago.

Success is peace of mind, which is a direct result of self-satisfaction in knowing you made the effort to do your best to become the best you are capable of becoming.

Now that's a definition.

One of the things I'm proudest of is my hunger for improvement. I was never one of the best footballers. And I know I'll never be the best orator, or the best psycholo-gist. There are very many sports psychologists around the world who are more knowledgeable and more qualified than me. But I can say that my appetite to learn and grow is immense.

So, looking back on those last three barren years of my inter-county career, certainly there were no honours. But did I try my best? Did I do everything in my power to become the best footballer I could possibly be?

Yes, I did.

And another thing – maybe if I had been a superstar for those three years, I'd be happy enough with where I am in my career. Today, I'm not happy enough. I'm driven to become the best that I'm capable of becoming.

And in that definition of success, there's my meaning. *To become the best I am capable of becoming.* Simple, but powerful enough to keep me going through all of the obstacles that get in my way.

Finally, a word about unrealistic optimism. You need to be optimistic, but it must be realistic optimism.

In the death camps, Viktor Frankl noted that the death rate in the week between Christmas 1944 and New Year's Day 1945 increased dramatically. The chief doctor at the camp told Frankl that he didn't believe that these deaths came as a result of harder working conditions, reduced supplies, harsher weather, illness or any other obvious cause. Rather, it was that so many of the prisoners had clung on to life in the naive hope that they would be home by Christmas.

Those who survived were the realistic optimists, the ones who didn't have any mystical confidence in a particular date but thought they had a reasonable chance of getting out in four or five years. Somehow, these people had the capacity to choose their own psychology and so could hold on to their sanity and give themselves the best chance of survival in the most desperate conditions.

Accomplishment

This is a funny one. Martin Seligman argues that, for many people, achieving just for the sake of it is a legitimate element of well-being. Though you'll rarely meet someone whose sense of well-being comes solely from the accumulation of wealth or status and nothing else, it is true that winning is the be-all and end-all for some people.

Some of us want to win *simply* to be the winner.

I like to think of the A in PERMA in another way. It's important to stop off and celebrate what you've *achieved*. When something goes well, you've got to acknowledge it. It's important to register the victories and say, *Yes, I got here, I did it!*

Celebrating micro-goals along the way has been shown to reduce cortisol levels – cortisol being the stress hormone. It also builds self-esteem and reduces self-doubt.

Celebrating little accomplishments along the way is critical to building your confidence.

'I've come this far! Why can't I go *here* now?'

10

RESILIENCE IN ACTION

The PERMA model might look great on paper. But how does it work in action?

I had a client, a very successful businessman, who ran a very successful multimillion-euro business. I got to know him through work we were doing in his organization. He was in his early fifties and married, with two grown-up children that he adored. One ordinary, unremarkable morning, his wife told him that she didn't love him any more and that the marriage was over. Just like that. Thirty years – over, with no warning. He did his best to convince her to stay, to make the relationship work. But within a couple of months, she had left him.

So began nearly two years of grief and turbulence. He felt useless and utterly alone. He blamed himself, he blamed her. He questioned everything about his life.

When he was finally ready to get himself out of the black pit into which he'd fallen, the first thing he did was turn to those around him. The R in the PERMA model. Relationships.

He already had a strong support structure available – his kids, his mother, his buddies, his work colleagues. Having zoned out for a long while, he reconnected with people and worked at nurturing his relationships, spending more time with the people who loved him, listening to them, talking to them, spending quality time with them. By feeling connected to these people, he began to turn things around and found the strength to fight his way back.

Here too is where he found meaning. He realized his life was all about family. He began to work towards making himself a better dad, a better son, a better friend.

As for positive emotions, he began a range of morning rituals designed to improve his psychology – the same ones I use all the time and that I detailed in Chapter 8, 'Eating, sleeping and staying on track': meditation, affirmations, gratitude work and Martin Seligman's 'What's Working Well' exercise. (Remember, this is a simple exercise where you write down three things that are working well in your life, along with the reason why each one is going well.)

Back in 2005, *Time* magazine ran a cover story on the big new thing in psychology – positive psychology, a field in which Martin Seligman is one of the leading lights. In anticipation of a big reaction, Seligman and his team at the University of Pennsylvania set up a website where members of the public could register and access the 'What's Working Well' exercise for free.

Thousands registered and took the happiness and depression tests on the site. Of that multitude, Seligman zeroed in on the fifty whose average depression score was 34, which put them in the category of 'extremely' depressed. These were people who could barely get out of bed in the morning. Everyone who registered agreed to do the WWW exercise for one week, then report back. Of those fifty, forty-seven tested as both significantly less depressed and significantly happier after seven days.

As Seligman acknowledges in *Flourish*, this was anything but a controlled study. However, subsequent scientific studies – which included placebos, random assignment, and so on – have generated similar results.

Another great exercise is 'One call a day' – resolving to make one call per day to someone you care about. A family member or a friend. A simple act like this helps to deepen relationships, build support structures and thereby increase your capacity for resilience.

Over about six years, my client worked on all the elements Seligman describes in his PERMA model and rebuilt his life. He began to take much better care of himself physically, and now he's in incredible shape for a man his age. He even took off around the world on his own for nine months, engaging with a new side of life and losing himself in the flow. (Admittedly, not something most of us are in a position to do!) And while he travelled, he kept up all the new routines he had introduced, and they continued to feed a very positive psychology. He continues to run a very successful business, and physically, emotionally and spiritually, he's in a great place.

What's your self-talk like?

Self-talk is the unspoken running commentary that we all conduct in our heads as we go about our daily lives, the internal voice that interprets every situation.

In times of adversity, self-talk can turn negative:

'I'm useless at this.'

'I never play well.'

'I'm going to make a mess of this again.'

These thoughts sabotage both your potential and your happiness.

Research tells us that simply being aware of negative self-talk goes a long way towards killing it. Keeping a journal is a great way to turn your attention to that small, insistent, negative voice.

Every day write down your most prominent thoughts, the things that are popping into your mind regularly. Now, start to critique them. Get a marker and put a red line under the negative and put a green line under the positive. Challenge the negative thoughts. Are these thoughts based on fact, or are they just negative interpretations? Are you jumping to conclusions?

> **TO KEEP YOUR PSYCHOLOGY POSITIVE, YOU NEED TO GET THE POSITIVE THOUGHTS TO OUTNUMBER THE NEGATIVE ONES.**

Various studies have shown that to keep your psychology positive, you need to get the positive thoughts to outnumber the negative ones by a ratio of five positive thoughts to every one negative thought. That's how powerful negative thoughts are. Monitoring your self-talk over a period of time will help you in achieving the right balance.

I met Christine Maloney about nine years ago, when I was working on a well-being programme in one of the banks. Christine was in a graduate role at the time, but it was easy to see that she had real ability. In the months following our first meeting, we met for coffee from time to time to discuss where she was at, and more particularly where she wanted to be.

One thing that became obvious was that while Christine had no problem critically analysing her performance, she didn't focus anything like as much attention on what she was doing well. I tried to explain the importance of positive affirm-ation and of aiming for a 5:1 ratio of positive to negative thoughts.

Christine admits she was sceptical at first.

'I worked in learning and development. I sat with people all day long doing development plans, delivering training ses-sions, working out needs analysis. That was how I was wired. I thought, "Sure, if I'm not aware of my development areas, I can't improve."'

I said that while she needed to be aware of areas for development, it was more important to understand and accept what she was really good at. She needed to be aware of what went well in her day, her week, her month.

'So I did as Enda suggested. Every morning, I'd write down the things that were going well, then I'd reflect on them. I'd pull them out at break, or pull them out before I went to bed. And then I began sticking them up in places where I'd see them. Up at the side of my bed, or on the mirror in my bathroom.'

For Christine, just repeating something positive about herself wasn't enough. The real power lay in writing it down.[4] Christine would list all of the things that were going well during her day, then name one – just one – area for

4 This is something that one of my earliest clients, David Gillick, used to do. In his wallet he even carried laminated copies of things he was proud of and grateful for. One day he went to pay in McDonald's and one of his affirmations fell out. He did a double take and said, 'You know what, actually, I won't have the Big Mac, I'll have a salad instead.'

development. All the time she kept that ratio of 5:1 at the front of her mind.

> 'I knew this approach was working simply because I began to feel much better about myself. People in work would say to me, "God, Christine, you're bouncing. You're in great form." And I was in great form, I was loving life.'

As the financial crisis began to bite, Christine was asked to work on a project restructuring the bank's leadership team. She helped to put about 400 people through a selection and development process and then chose 70 from among that group who would rebuild the internal structure of the bank. It was a major project that demanded long hours and removed her from the people she'd worked with for years.

There was no extra pay or clarity about her promotion prospects when it was over. In addition, this was at a time when the reputation of banks and bankers could not have been worse, so Christine knew she was working in a sector the public despised.

> 'All that work I had done on positivity, that's when it started to pay off. I was able to look at what I was doing in a totally different light. I could see that despite all the negative stuff, this was an amazing opportunity. I was twenty-five and I was being asked to chair a selection process with the board of the bank. I may not have known where I was going in terms of salary or promotion, I may have been working flat out, but I was getting loads of exposure and learning huge amounts. Plus I was really enjoying what I was doing.'

Once again, we're back to mindset. These positivity exercises helped to focus Christine on the learning opportunity rather than the crisis.

When it was all over, she landed a serious promotion, actually skipping a grade to enter her new role – not something that happens regularly in a business as hierarchical as banking.

'I was told afterwards that one of the reasons I nailed that promotion was because of the mindset I had during those tough times. I was the one going around saying, "This is a great opportunity. We could make a difference here."'

Resilience in the moment

A sudden crisis hits.

The crucial thing to do is step back. Even if it's only for five minutes. Or a minute. Or thirty seconds.

Find even a moment to catch your breath. Become aware of your breathing. Try to calm everything down and create a clear headspace so you can think.

This is the time to step back and ask yourself:

'OK, how am I going to react here?'

'How do I respond to this problem?'

'What is the best possible strategy?'

You are faced with a stimulus, the situation is about to spin out of control. What happens next is your choice.

Do you collapse, or do you manage it?

This is when you choose to say, 'OK, I'm going to deal with this in a composed manner. I'm going to figure out the first thing I need to do. And the thing I need to do after that. And what I should do in the next hour or so. Other people are panicking, so I'm going to keep my head as best I can and behave in a controlled way. I know I can manage my mind and draw on my reserves of resilience to get through this. I can keep my emotions in check for the moment. There will be a safe and appropriate time when I can release my emotions. But for now, I'm going to handle myself.'

Once you've chosen your psychology, you then choose your strategy.

It's like a surgeon deciding, 'What we're going to do is, we're going to put in a valve immediately.'

Or the Gaelic footballer in Croke Park deciding that their man might have scored 1-5, but if he can get one more tackle in, they might still win this game.

Or the CEO deciding that, even though the stock price is tanking, the current strategy will continue because it's the best long-term strategy for the company.

Or it's Nelson Mandela on the plane, seeing no sense in panic.

Or it's my mother, deciding that, yes, something bad has happened, something terrible has happened, but hysteria won't help.

We are calm.

We get on with things.

RESILIENCE – TAKE ACTION NOW!

1. *Practise choosing your psychology.* For the next week make a commitment that you will stand back and reflect on any setback or any hardship that comes your way and that you will reflect on how you choose to respond. Challenge yourself to choose your response to the adversity.

2. *Try Martin Seligman's WWW exercise every night this week.* Just before you drift off to sleep think about what's working well in your life. Spend time making a mental note of each one.

3. *Monitor your self-talk for the next week.* In a journal write down the prominent negative thoughts and positive thoughts that you have. At the end of the week critique this journal and analyse which of the thoughts are going to help you live the life you want to live and which are going to hold you back.

4. *Over the next week contact one friend a day.* Really engage with them. If you can, go and meet them. Aim to really connect with them.

MENTAL STRENGTH

11

COMFORTABLE IN THE COLISEUM

Not only does my mother share Nelson Mandela's coolness under pressure but, like him, she was also on a plane when one of its engines failed. She was on a flight from Dublin to London. When the plane was eighty feet in the air, one of the engines ruptured. The plane pitched to one side and the wing almost hit the ground. The pilot managed to right it before disaster struck, but clearly they were not yet out of the woods. The pilot called the flight attendants into the cockpit. When my mother saw them walking back down the aisle of the plane, she knew from their faces that things were very serious.

Everyone went into crash positions as the pilot flew the plane out over the Irish Sea to dump fuel.

Within fifteen minutes, he had guided the plane back to the airport and landed safely.

Afterwards, the passengers discovered that one of the fuel lines had been exposed right at the site of the damaged engine – which was hanging off the wing. Had the two made contact, the whole thing would have gone up in smoke.

So all's well that ends well, with one exception – my father.

Mum had been going to London for the weekend. Dad had brought her to the airport and waited – as he always did – until he saw her plane accelerating down the runway. Then he turned and headed towards the exit.

He had barely made it to the door of the terminal building when he heard sirens and saw flashing lights. Suddenly the entire place was gripped by panic, with people running everywhere. When he grabbed someone to find out what was the matter, they were in too much of a rush to respond. Of course, later he found out the whole story.

The story of the near-crash at Dublin Airport was big news for a few days, not least because the broadcaster Gay Byrne had been on board. Dad was an English teacher at the time, and the kids in his class were fascinated with the whole thing. They would ask, over and over again, to hear the story of the plane that nearly crashed, and Dad – being a great storyteller – would tell them. And each time he told them, the story became more dramatic.

The problem was that with each retelling, my father was beginning to frighten himself. It got to a point where, if he looked up into the sky and saw an aeroplane, he would begin to feel nervous. Though he had never been an anxious flyer, the experience now became terrifying.

'That was 1984,' he says. 'For the next ten years, I didn't get on a plane. There were several opportunities to go over to England for weddings and things like that, and I always said, "No, I'm not going. I'm just not going."'

Dad's flight simulator

The problem that confronted my father is one that confronts millions of people every day. I'm not talking about the fear of flying, specifically, but being mentally unable to do something that you're more than capable of doing physically. It's not as if my dad couldn't walk up the steps of the aeroplane, it was merely that he had acquired a fear that made it mentally repugnant to him to do so.

The irony is that Dad was deeply aware of the workings of the human mind. When I was a kid, we had an old, green, battered Renault 18 that spent most of its life ferrying gangs of lads to and from matches. It had blue seats, but the driver's seat must have been replaced at some point because it was grey. And in this battered, green Renault 18, there was your standard radio cassette player – ours was held in place with matchsticks. Dad always played the one tape. It was from a series of lectures called 'Investment in Excellence' by an American mentor and motivational guru, Lou Tice. As a kid, of course, I had no time for this stuff. *That bloody tape? Again?!*

Looking back now, I realize that more than anyone else, my father is the reason why I am in this profession. He's the reason our company exists, and why I have a lifelong passion for psychology and unlocking people's potential.

Dad understood the importance of mental preparation and mental toughness long before any of his contemporaries. He has a degree in psychology and has been tuning into the latest developments in this area for as long as I can remember. He also coached football teams for most of his life. The fact that he prepared his teams so well mentally was a big factor in the success he had over the years.

Anyway, cut to ten years after the incident at Dublin Airport. Dad has changed career and is now working as a development consultant with a community group in Newry on an economic regeneration project set up during the Northern Ireland peace process. He recognized that the group was lacking in self-belief and thought he might be able to do something about it.

He explains:

'They were locked into the idea that "We can't do stuff". Their horizons were so low that it was very difficult to inspire them to think. In the meantime, I had been on the Investment in Excellence course in Belfast three times. It was all about changing behaviours, releasing untapped potential, motivating yourself and accepting accountability. I thought it would stimulate the realization that "Hang on, we're not as bad as we thought we were."'

So Dad went and secured funding for the course, then organized a facilitator to come over from London to run it. Then, at the last minute, the facilitator got sick and couldn't travel.

'I was on the phone to the organizer in Manchester, trying to work out what our options were. He said to me, "You do it. You were a teacher, you've been on the course three times, you could do it." He told me that they gave two days of training to their facilitators, and that these training courses were run every weekend, and that I should just come over and do the course. Of course, then I said, "I've a bit of a problem there. I don't fly." He said, "You don't fly? And you're doing this stuff?"'

The organizer put it up to Dad. He told him that he would book the flight for one month's time. If Dad really believed in the material – if he believed that it was possible to change his perception and dump a fear that was holding him back – he would get on that plane in four weeks.

Dad took the challenge. He sat down and began putting all he had learned into practice. This started with drafting what he calls his 'trigger sentence'.

'Instead of looking at the reality of now, where I'm frightened out of my life by flying, I asked myself, "What would it be like if it was fixed?" In other words, what's my goal? So I wrote down, "I am thrilled that I can now get on a plane to London and be relaxed and calm." It has to be present tense, and you have to get emotion into it. Again: "I am thrilled that I can now get on a plane to London and be relaxed and calm."'

With that trigger sentence in place, the next step was to begin simulating the flight. They train pilots by putting them into flight simulators, where every aspect of flying a plane is minutely reproduced. The pilot only gets access to a real plane once he has mastered the simulator. Dad set out to create his own flight simulator, but entirely within his mind. This process is about recreating the sensory experience of getting on an aeroplane and flying, without actually doing it.

'I see it happening. I see myself walking along that gangway into the plane, I hear the noise of it. Now, straight away, I hear the sound of the engine and start to feel it beneath my feet, and I start to get the collywobbles. I'm moving down the aisle, looking for my seat. The nervousness is there, but I know what my goal is. My goal is to be sitting in that seat nice and calm as the plane takes off.'

He had, of course, been on loads of flights before, so he had the advantage of knowing what the process of taking a flight was like. He knew how the fabric of the seat felt under his skin, he knew what the air felt like. He could put himself right inside the experience by closing his eyes and imagining it.

'It's like producing a video. I visualize what's happening around me, the people getting into their seats, putting baggage in the overhead compartments, I see the flight attendants smiling and helping people, I hear the announcements over the intercom. And now everyone is sitting and we're taxiing down the runway, I can feel the collywobbles intensify, I feel the movement of the plane as it's trundling along, then it turns on to the runway and I feel the seat press into my back as it accelerates.'

THE SUBCONSCIOUS MIND DOESN'T KNOW THE DIFFERENCE BETWEEN REALITY AND A WELL-ACTED VISUALIZATION.

Emotion is essential to an exercise like this. You act the part of someone taking a flight without the fear, and because the subconscious mind doesn't know the difference between reality and a well-acted visualization, the fear of flying nervous is supplanted by the imagined experience of flying calm.

The first time Dad sat down to put himself through this process, the whole thing took just two minutes, from start to finish. After that, each full simulation took barely a minute. Nor did he need to go to a quiet space to do it, he just took the opportunity whenever it presented itself – in the shower, going for a walk, whatever. Ten times each day for the following fourteen days, he repeated the simulation. This pattern, the course facilitator had suggested, would be sufficient to embed the new way of thinking.

For the last two weeks before the flight, Dad didn't do anything to tackle his fear of flying. But because he had generated those visualizations so frequently over the previous fortnight, they popped back into his head regularly throughout that time.

When he got to the airport, he had no idea if any of this had worked or not.

Then, as he was on his way up the steps of the plane, an elderly woman turned to him and said, 'Son, would you mind if I held your hand on the flight, because I'm terrified of flying.'

Dad didn't tell her anything about his own state of mind. He just said, 'OK.'

'Once on the plane, we got into a conversation. I mean, when you're holding somebody's hand and you've never met them before, that's a pretty good trigger for a conversation. So I said, "You tell me about you." And that's what the flight consisted of. She told me her life story. And it was one of the most interesting stories I'd ever heard. I can't remember a word of it now, but I was so taken up with her story, I never even thought of the flight.'

You could argue that the distraction of talking to that woman was what enabled Dad to take that flight without fear. But she wasn't there on the way home, and he was fine.

Shortly after, he had another flight, to Madrid, and wasn't so good on that flight because he hadn't prepared: 'The following year, I had a fifteen-hour flight to San Francisco and the plane was full to the neck. I did my preparations before-hand and I was fine. And I've been fine ever since.'

The one thing Dad is keen to point out is that there's noth-ing mystical about this transformation. This was simply a process of accelerated learning. By recreating the event, over and over again, as he did, he displaced the original imprint of the experience with a fresh conception of it in which fear had been replaced with calm.

Taking control

What my father was doing with his flight simulation exer-cises was taking control. Rather than allowing himself to be led by his fear, he chose a new psychology for himself and learned the mental strength to overcome the thing that was holding him back.

Today, much of the work we do in McNulty Performance is about helping clients to learn the mental toughness that will enable them to perform to the best of their ability. It can be anything – a big match, an impor-tant speech, an interview, a live TV show, a major performance – but no matter what it is, the thing that determines success more than any other is being comfortable. Success comes from being so comfortable that you are absolutely at home and therefore capable of performing to your potential. So comfort-able that you can get into the zone and stay there.

THE THING THAT DETERMINES SUCCESS MORE THAN ANY OTHER IS BEING COMFORTABLE.

If you watch the elite of the elite perform – if you watch them forensically before, during and after the performance – you will see that they have a lot in common. They walk with poise and appear calm and composed. They seem to have loads of time. They may even have a half-smile on their face. When the intensity is raised and the stakes are heightened, it's as if they press the slow-motion button.

And that's mental toughness.

Mental toughness is being confident, composed, disciplined and concentrated when faced with adversity and when under pressure.

All the great performers are mentally tough. I love watching elite performers perform the basic skills consistently well, and execute the extraordinary skills on big occasions in a packed stadium.

Robbie Henshaw, the young Irish and Leinster player, is a great example of someone who works consistently on his mental toughness. He is absolutely at home when he plays, and he plays with such ease, oblivious of the circumstances, completely in the zone.

Roger Federer is one of the greatest examples of an athlete who could show up and perform like this, time after time.

Padraic Moyles did it over 5,000 times with *Riverdance*.

Brian O'Driscoll became one of the best in the world at producing his finest performance just when his team needed him most.

The Williams sisters have dominated women's tennis for over ten years thanks to their physical and mental strength.

Being mentally strong is absolutely essential in competition.

Lots of people have the athletic make-up, the skill, the talent, the fitness to excel in their field. But finding a way to be comfortable in the white heat of battle – to be comfortable in the Coliseum – that's the big differentiator.

When you have found a way to be comfortable you have a major advantage.

When Armagh played Kerry in the 2000 All-Ireland semi-final, I was marking Mike Frank Russell, a brilliant footballer. I remember, at one point he kicked a ball from 21 yards out. I was standing at the goalpost. The ball literally dribbled over the line into the goal. Even now, I can't quite believe it. But I just stood and watched. Picture it: I'm standing there, on the goal line, and all I have to do is walk – walk, never mind sprint! – and I do nothing.

I was so hijacked by the occasion, I couldn't move. I was like a bunny caught in the headlights, watching this ball dribble into the goal and rob us of a crack at the All-Ireland final.

So was I comfortable at Croke Park at the start?

Definitely not.

But I worked hard on my mental strength. I worked on it so much that I knew I had won the mental battle with my direct opponent before the game began. Looking into his eyes at the handshake before the game, I could tell that I had a mental edge. I knew when I went for the first ball that my opponent would be worried about the consequences.

My role on the team was not sexy. I was not doing the silky stuff. My job was always to target the most dangerous player from the opposition team and prevent him from scoring. To do that, you always have to perform at a high level. If you are even 10% off, you will get wiped out.

I performed consistently at the level the team needed. However, with the benefit of hindsight, I can see that I had much more potential than I realized. I had so much more to offer, if I had known then what I know now.

12

GETTING TOUGH

The roots of my mental toughness go back to when I first started to play football seriously at secondary school, in Newry. The pitch we used to train on was one of the worst pitches in the country. The school has moved since, and the pitch is now overgrown, but I was back in Newry recently and jumped a fence to take a look at it. It's actually more of a bowl than a pitch. And during the winter, it was muck and gutters – you wouldn't put cattle on it. And yet that miserable little pitch produced so many All-Ireland winners and All Stars for both Down and Armagh.

Val Kane was our PE teacher and Gaelic football coach. Val was a small, powerfully built man, with a voice that you could hear halfway across town. He had played for the great Down teams of the 1960s. In his training techniques, Val was ahead of his time. He'd have the following day's training session up on the noticeboard in the corridor (similar to how the Irish rugby team does things today) – how many runs we were going to do, how much time would be spent on skills, the session's specific focus, goals of the session, and so on. He would also tell us on the Monday before a big game to begin to work on our mental preparation for the weekend.

What I liked most about him was that he challenged the life out of me. There was never a session where I wasn't stretched – mentally, physically, technically and tactically. Because it wasn't just about the physical side of the game. He got us to think about mental toughness, and then he would show us how to develop it.

There was a room below the gym where he took us for PE Studies. (We were very fortunate that we could choose Physical Education as a subject to study at 'A' level.) I was fascinated in those classes, as Val educated us about the politics of sport, the sociology of sport, and of course the psychology of sport. I remember Val standing at the head of the class, lecturing us on the concept of the total athlete and telling us about Pierre de Coubertin, the father of the modern Olympics. As he talked, you could hear basketballs slapping the floor of the gym overhead.

There were four future All-Ireland winners in that room, as well as me – John and Tony McEntee, Aidan O'Rourke and Barry Duffy. My brother Justin, Kieran McGeeney and Cathal O'Rourke had also been through Val's school of excellence.

I can draw a red line from what happened in that room to what I achieved on the pitch with Armagh, and right through to what I'm now doing for a living. Val gave us an awareness and understanding of everything, from the psychology of sport to the practicalities of drawing up a long-term training plan.

Programming physical and mental toughness

Val put a huge emphasis on physical fitness, and strength in particular. We were in the gym doing strength work three times a week. By any standards, our fitness levels were incredible. By the time I was fifteen, I could squat 120kg.

Val knew and understood the value of playing to your strengths, and he worked hard to help me develop mine. I remember, at a training session on that unplayable pitch, a ball came in between me and another guy. It was his ball – he should have won it – but at the last second, I dived in over him and got my fist to it. Val stopped the session, ran over and brought everyone in, then spent about two minutes praising me for my bravery, for my hunger to get to the ball, for my controlled aggression. That's something you don't forget when you're thirteen.

When I was playing Under-14 for my local club, Mullaghbawn, the guy who managed the team asked me to take the training sessions.

He said, 'Listen, I don't know that much about coaching. You play for the local school team, you're playing at a high level. You train the team.'

So I did.

I just copied what I'd seen Val and our other coach, Jim McCartan, do.

My father was the coach of the senior team, and when they were short of some players he would throw me in. Training with the senior team wasn't just about being physically capable of doing what they did. It was also about having the temperament to mix it with the older guys. You can't hang around with a group of hardened senior club footballers from South Armagh and not know how to handle yourself. Or you'd get eaten alive. In the dressing room at half-time, when the opposition is taking you to the cleaners, you've got to be able to cope with that.

And you need to be prepared for the going to get ugly sometimes too. I recall my dad coming home from a match when I was small and Mum saying to him, 'What happened to your coat, Joe?' It was ripped to shreds. He shrugged and said he'd had to block the corridor after the match, because the other team wanted to get into the dressing room to fight the Mullaghbawn lads. This was South Armagh. You got incidents like that from time to time.

One Sunday morning, I was with Dad at a challenge match and one of our players showed up badly hung-over. Dad said, 'I'm not going with him. I'm going to put Enda in there.' There would have been opposition – I was still only fourteen – but Dad didn't care.

I played, and played well. I won a lot of ball.

The next Sunday, he threw me in again. And again. Eventually, I got the respect of the senior players, who said, 'Stick Enda in at corner forward.'

Even though I was young, it didn't mean the opposition was going to let me have an easy game. I was still just fifteen when a guy I was marking said to me, 'If you go for the next ball, I'm going to break your leg.' I went for the ball anyway, and while I can't say he tried to break my leg, he certainly tried to hurt me. So the opposition were absolutely going to get stuck in. That was the nature of that league.

I used to run in all weathers, in all conditions. Sometimes with one of my brothers, either Justin or Paul, and sometimes with some of my teammates. But a lot of the time I was on my own. I would repeat these affirmations as I ran:

'Every day in every way, I'm getting stronger and stronger.'

'Playing football to my full potential is something I achieve on an ongoing basis.'

'I'm strong, I'm teak-tough, I'm a leader.'

'Under pressure, I always step up.'

'I stay composed. I stay calm.'

And then I'd think about the future, and I'd repeat these mantras, over and over and over again, as I ran:

'I look forward to being in Croke Park on the third Sunday in September, to winning the All-Ireland.'

'I look forward to being on an Armagh team that wins an All-Ireland.'

I might pause the run to do press-ups, then challenge myself to run to the top of the hill without stopping.

I would tell myself, *Never let your mind tell you your body's tired.*

NEVER LET YOUR MIND TELL YOU YOUR BODY'S TIRED.

This was halfway up the mountain. Nobody was watching, nobody but me. But I was programming myself. Every day, I was programming myself to be mentally tough. Even as a teenager I realized that toughness of the mind and toughness of the body are part of the same continuum, and that they share many of the same markers. I understood that all of this would give me a competitive advantage. While others would capitulate under pressure, I would be ice-cool.

I would be able to handle the pressure better than anyone else.

Dragging a tyre over the mountains

A guy called Brian Bell got in touch with the company a few years back. He was an ordinary guy – an ex-garda, married with two children and living in Annagassan, Co. Louth – but he had an extraordinary ambition. He wanted to do the Yukon Arctic Ultra. This is probably the toughest race in the world. It's certainly the coldest – a 300-mile trek through a frozen wasteland, with temperatures reaching as low as –40°C.

One of the team in the office picked up Brian's email and mailed him back with details of our services, fee structure, and so on. Brian responded with a phone call. 'No, no,' he said, 'you misunderstand me. I don't want to pay for anything. I just want to talk to Enda.'

I agreed to meet Brian in Bewley's on Grafton Street. There, he elaborated:

'For this to be of any value to me, I have to feel that you're interested in what I'm doing. You can go anywhere and get anything if you just pay the money, but for me, I need someone to validate the intensity of what I'm doing. Money can't be involved, or it won't work.'

He explained a bit more about the race. The course was over 300 miles through thick snow and forest, over frozen lakes and across uninhabited wasteland. He would have to survive on two hours' sleep per night as he dragged his sled through the wilderness.

Recalling the challenge, Brian says:

'I would be pretty strong mentally, but this was different. I would be on my own for days at a time in one of the most inhospitable places on earth. To keep self-motivated, and to keep safe, I knew I needed help.'

It tells you something about the extreme nature of the race that just eighteen people were due to start. Moreover, the drop-out rate is huge. Fewer than half tend to finish.

While it was open to teams of two, Brian was going to do it solo, which made things twice as tough and twice as dangerous.

> 'If there's two of you and you hit a bad spell, the other guy can go in front and make trail. Everybody has ups and downs, but when you're on your own, you don't have that back-up. You're crossing lakes up there for twenty or thirty hours at a time. A team can rope up in case anyone goes through. But when you're on your own and you fall, you're gone.'

We agreed to get involved, so I got the team together and we began working through Brian's plan. His focus and determination were already exceptional. The training regime he'd put himself through was gruelling. In the depths of an Irish winter, he'd wait for a weather warning, then head out into the Cooley Mountains. With the wind driving freezing rain into his face, he'd tether himself to a tyre and pull it through the night.

As the race approached, Brian's mental preparation stepped up a gear and he began the process of controlling everything that could be controlled. Like Dad before he boarded the aeroplane Brian began working on his visualizations. But he had never been to any of the places he would see during the race, and he had no prior experience to draw sensory data from.

> 'I did Google searches and YouTube searches of specific checkpoints, so that I would know what they looked like. That way, when I was on my own at four in the morning, I could build a profile of the next checkpoint in my mind: what it would look like, who would be there, what they were

going to give me. My food rations were individually pack-
aged for each checkpoint, so I would know, for example,
that at Checkpoint 4, my treat would be Turkish Delight.'

We examined each stage of the route in minute detail,
teasing out which ones would be the most challenging, which
ones he would need special preparation for, and coming up
with strategies to soften those challenges. There were six different checkpoints on the race, and all of them, understandably,
had local names. Dog Grave Lake was one, Deadman's Cove
was another. To increase the number of things that Brian
had control over, we came up with the idea of renaming
those checkpoints. Instead of Dog Grave Lake and
Deadman's Cove, he used the names of his children.

There was one stage in particular that we could see was
going to be especially tough. It was long and utterly deserted,
and this was where most of the competitors tended to drop
out. That one, Brian named after his late father.

'You wouldn't believe how much that helped. I know it
sounds a bit flowery now, but it really, really worked. You're
at a stage of the race that you've articulated as being very
dangerous, where the drop-out rate is huge, but instead of
being anxious about it, you take control of it with a personal
name. It's almost like a trigger word. Now, all of a sudden,
it's your stage, it's Dad, it's my son, it's my daughter, and
nothing will stop me from getting there. As I stand here in
lovely, sunny Annagassan it sounds a bit extreme, but I was
in a very extreme situation. What will motivate you here
won't motivate you at minus forty, when you haven't seen
anyone in three days, and you're hoping you're not going to
go through the ice.'

To further sweeten the deal, Brian got his kids to write him letters, each of which would be waiting for him at the checkpoints he had named for them. Alone in the snow, the knowledge that there was a letter from his daughter waiting for him sixty miles down the trail was a huge motivator.

Central to Brian's approach was an understanding that, to prepare for any kind of demanding event, you must accept that physical and mental preparation are interdependent.

It's important to get your head in the right place.

When I played with Armagh during those breakthrough years, not only was our physical fitness training exceptional, we *knew* it was exceptional. We knew that we were becoming the fittest team in the country. It's one thing to be that, it's another to walk out on an Ulster final or an All-Ireland semi-final and *know* it in your bones.

Our conditioning games contributed substantially to the team's mental toughness. We used to do two-minute tackling exercises in a grid the size of a small room – three metres by three metres. If you do that seven or eight times a session, it's going to toughen you. Mentally, you're focused on the skill you need to execute the tackles, the passes, the catches. You have to keep making decisions under pressure, at moments when you're physically exhausted and half battered.

That's mental fitness: making decisions properly under pressure, over and over and over again.

Brian didn't engage in the lunacy of dragging a tyre over the Cooley Mountains just to get physically fit. He also did it to know that he could do it. When he was struggling along that remote

MENTAL FITNESS IS MAKING DECISIONS PROPERLY UNDER PRESSURE, OVER AND OVER AND OVER AGAIN.

trail, halfway between nowhere and nowhere else, he could replay the misery of leaving the fire and heading out into a storm on the Cooleys and know that mentally he was toughened. Remember, toughness of the mind and toughness of the body are part of the same continuum.

To help him connect with that experience, Brian used a kind of walking meditation. We applied the same techniques that we had used for Ian McKeever in his quest to conquer Everest. Brian would practise walking tall, focusing on one breath and one step at a time; rather than focusing on the pain, he was focusing on his breath, and the step.

> 'If you're going through a bad point where you're getting really tired and you need to keep the pace up, you almost force yourself to stop thinking about the pain in your feet from the cold, or the fact that your eyes are stinging. So I focused on my breathing. I got intensely focused on each inhale and on each exhale. I got focused on each step. You still feel the pain, but it's not as strong. It's like there is an alarm going off in the building but you are listening to classical music. I also visualized the training I did at home. I could spend a couple of hours reliving the things I'd done, the routes I'd taken up in the mountains, the things I'd seen. I drew all the strength and energy out of that until I began to feel better about where I was.'

In the previous section on resilience, I talked about the PERMA model and how the most resilient people have great support networks. We are a social species, we have evolved to depend on one another. When we have strong social support, we are much more resilient.

But what about in the middle of Yukon?

Brian's experience of isolation during that race tells you a lot about just how fundamental human contact is.

'I met a trapper once, one of the First Nation, as they call the indigenous people up there. I calculated afterwards that I hadn't seen a human in fifty-four hours. I'm in the middle of a forest and he's looking at me and I'm looking at him. It's about minus forty-odd. I unhooked my sled, went over and stuck out my hand. He said, "Man, what the hell are you doing here?" I told him I was heading to Dawson. He said, "You're crazy." I said, "Yeah, I know." He'd never heard of Europe, let alone Ireland. For the next fifteen minutes or so, I talked the arse off him. I wrecked him with talk, and as I talked, I could feel the energy surging back into me. I'd never realized just how challenging it is being on your own.'

Of the eighteen people who started the race, just seven finished. Brian came third overall, behind two teams of two, and ahead of one other pair, which is unheard of. He was the only individual to finish. Since then, he's gone on to compete in the 250-kilometre Marathon des Sables across the Sahara Desert, and recently the 230-kilometre Jungle Ultra Marathon in Peru.

'I haven't ever done anything as challenging as the jungle race before. It's just brutal in there. Wherever you go, there's something that wants to bite you. In the Arctic, it's dangerous but beautiful. You can appreciate where you are, whereas in the jungle it's just head down the whole time. Every river crossing you make, you come out with a leech attached to you somewhere, trying to get his grub. There are snakes and bullet ants, flying ants, caiman, piranha . . .'

At fifty-two years of age, Brian was the oldest competitor in the race, but still managed to come ninth, beating dozens of guys who, on paper at least, should have left him standing. There were ex-SAS, ex-Foreign Legion, guys born into that environment ten and fifteen years younger than him.

'I'm just a fifty-something dad. I'm nobody compared to the people Enda deals with, and yet I'm able to go to an environment I've had no experience of and compete strongly in there against people who have tons of experience. That comes down to one thing only – what's going on upstairs.

'You can train, you can run and you can be the fittest guy in the world. But if you haven't done the mental training, don't get on the plane – all your preparation will be worthless. It's the guy who's still thinking straight, the guy who has a strategy, who has the mental toughness, he's the guy who'll come through. It's all down to the mental stuff.'

13

THINK YOUR WAY INTO BETTER PERFORMANCE

A 2012 research project conducted by a team of Italian and German academics tells us a lot about how effective mental rehearsal can be. Sixteen pianists, ranging in age from eighteen to thirty-six, were given two pieces of music to learn. To compare mental practice with physical practice, the group was divided in two, and rehearsals were scheduled on alternate days. On the first day, half of the pianists engaged in half an hour of mental rehearsal *only*, then performed the pieces from memory, while the other half practised physically and, once again, performed the pieces from memory.

So what did they find?

In the performance after the mental practice, the musicians were able to get through 63% of the rehearsal before being unable to recall any more. The physical rehearsal proved more effective, with pianists getting to the 84% mark before having to stop. The researchers also measured the number of mistakes made, concluding again that physical practice was more effective.

The interesting finding, however, was that when both groups were given an additional ten minutes' *physical* practice, *all* performed to the same standard. In other words, those who practised mentally for thirty minutes and physically for ten minutes played as well as those who had practised for forty minutes physically.

On his website, bulletproofmusician.com, the musician and performance psychologist Noa Kageyama cites this and other studies which show the growing evidence that mental practice can make a significant difference to performance.

Use a mental rehearsal script

Brian Bell couldn't train on the Yukon Trail. (Nor could he head into the Amazon jungle a month before the race in order to prepare.) All he had was a tyre, a few YouTube videos of the terrain and the Cooley Mountains. He had to be creative about how he trained mentally. We collaborated and created a mental toughness training plan, and he executed it better than the vast majority of athletes I work with. I guess he knew that he had to – if he was mentally weak, he was in danger of freezing to death in the snow.

Brian began to mentally rehearse all possible scenarios on the Yukon Trail. He mentally rehearsed what the loneliness would be like; how his hands would feel; what his face would feel like with the bitterness of the cold on his beard. A couple of times a day he went through it all in his mind and imagined what it would feel like.

And it worked.

But you don't have to be preparing for a big adventure to benefit from this technique.

Suppose you have an important event coming up – say, giving a presentation at your company's sales conference.

Preparing a mental rehearsal script will help you. For the next twenty-one days, lie on your sofa, put on relaxing music, focus on your breathing for three to four minutes, then read this script.

> 'I am confident, composed, and calm under pressure. I really enjoy performing to my full potential. I love performing in front of a big crowd. I am ready to perform to the best of my ability. I am completely engaged in the process when I perform. I use my breathing to regulate my mind during my performance. I am ready. I love performing under pressure . . .'

And so on.

Write down – in the present tense – everything that you know will happen, all of your interactions, all the things that you will say, how you will engage with people. Write it all out in the most vivid detail you can imagine, ensuring that you embed positive emotion into every element.

Once your script is written, use it to guide your rehearsal, to keep you focused.

Simulate real-life situations

In Chapter 6, 'Staying the distance', I talked about the former Leinster rugby player Bernard Jackman, and the throwing practice he used to develop his skills. I want to go into a little more depth here about the quality of his mental and physical preparations at that time. It was this work, I believe, that contributed hugely to the great year he had in 2008, culminating with his being awarded Player of the Year in Leinster.

Bernard says:

'Throwing wasn't something that I ever mastered. It wasn't something that came naturally. Genetically, I had really limited flexibility in my shoulder and neck joints. That protected me from shoulder injuries but the downside was that it limited my throwing range.'

What he needed was to get throwing to the best possible level that he could get it to; the rest of his game was easily good enough to get him into the team.

There was nothing I could tell Bernard about technique – any more than I could tell Padraic Moyles about dancing, or Brian Bell about pulling a sled. What I could do is help to get him into the right mental state to throw consistently, regardless of the circumstances.

'A goal kicker has a routine. He goes through that identical routine every time he takes a place kick. A hooker needs something similar. Those "simulator" sessions with Enda were all about developing the skills to execute my routine in the exact same way every time, regardless of what else is going on in the game. Trying to get into the zone, in other words, regardless of whether I was playing well or badly, to not let any distractions affect my capacity to carry out that task.'

Bernard and I did sessions where I had him hitting bags or doing sprints, then back to the line for a throw. We tried to simulate exactly the movements, the calls, the positioning on the pitch, the physicality, the mental challenge that Bernard would face during a match. We would try to simulate real-life situations.

I would say, 'We're three points down, inside the Toulouse twenty-two. We're in the red zone. You're after missing a tackle one minute ago. The crowd are going absolutely crazy. Line-out. Step-up. Throw.'

That endless repetition, the process of continually creating the conditions of the upcoming challenge, were an attempt to make the real thing as fluid and as natural as possible. When he arrived in a match situation and had to throw, all that work resolved itself into a series of movements that were as familiar to him as breathing.

Of course, those line-out sessions were just one element of a plan. Bernard's preparation covered everything from nutrition, strength and conditioning, to energy management, rest and recovery and mental training. He couldn't control the weather on match day, or the size of the crowd, or the strength of the opposition. But everything he could control, he did.

'Goal-setting and performance-planning were a big part of the work we did. Each week, we worked out a set of targets for each game, a set of specific things I would aim for. Where that really helped was in cutting the distractions, cutting the things I didn't need to focus on. It gave me an awful lot more clarity getting ready for match day. I would then work on a plan for the week, and that would focus me on what the four or five key aspects of my preparation were.'

We broke the plan down into all of the things Bernard needed to do to make sure he was going to perform. That might be any number of things – a yoga session, a massage, eating right, an extra video session, getting an extra hour's sleep.

'That alone made you confident; knowing that you had prepared differently than you had in the past. In the dressing room before I went out, I knew what I had to do very, very specifically, in a sort of micromanaged way. And as each week went by, that process built and fed that confidence.'

And, as Bernard points out, preparation gets you into the right frame of mind ahead of the performance, dampening down what my father would call 'the collywobbles'.

'If you know exactly what you need to bring on Saturday, the earlier in the week that you accept that and start to prepare mentally for the sacrifice that's going to be needed, the more ready you are to play. And in the warm-up in the dressing room before the game, there's less anxiety because you feel, "OK, I know what I'm about. I know what I need to do. I've prepped for it." And you just want to get out there and do it.'

Focus on your strengths

Another critical element of Bernard Jackman's game-day strategy lay in playing to his strengths. Now a coach himself – of FC Grenoble, in France – he believes that the best thing any player can do for his team is to execute what he does well.

'Don't try to pull a rabbit out of a hat, don't worry about stuff that doesn't concern you. Just understand what strength you bring to the team as a player, and then, in those tough moments, make sure that that's what you're concentrating on.'

Greatness in any player comes from the fact that he or she does the ordinary things extraordinarily well. Yes, sometimes you'll see flashes of wizardry, but most of the time, their brilliance lies in simply playing to their strengths.

Brian O'Driscoll is a guy I have learned a massive amount from. He is probably one of the most mentally tough athletes I have witnessed or worked with. He had the great ability to show up at the show-down time after time.

Brian has spoken publicly about the shift in his thinking in regard to the importance of mental training. In the 2008–09 season, he committed to and delivered a great shift in his mental approach. It began when I got a call from Michael Cheika, the Leinster head coach.

He said, 'Listen, Enda, I want you to come in and talk to Brian. He's not . . .'

Cheika didn't finish the sentence, but I knew from watching Brian in successive games that he wasn't playing even close to his potential. For someone who could dazzle you on the pitch, he clearly wasn't himself.

I met Brian in Michael Cheika's office in Riverview, the Leinster training base. Brian was sitting deep in an armchair, hood up, hands in his pockets. Michael sat in with us for a few minutes, then he left, and I began talking to Brian.

I asked him to tell me where he was at. He told me he wasn't enjoying his rugby. He felt very negative about himself. He knew that he wasn't close to his potential, he felt that he was past his sell-by date, and that his rugby career was fast coming to an end.

'Tell me about your self-talk, Brian, what's that like?'

He told me it was predominantly negative. He said that when he looked back over his rugby games, all he could see was negativity, all he could see were the things that had gone wrong. He was worried about injuries, about losing his pace.

I listened to him and started untangling his thoughts, trying to identify what was holding him back.

We didn't progress too far in that first session, but the second time I met him he was noticeably more open. He had clearly decided he wanted to shift how he mentally prepared, how he approached the game in general.

All change ultimately begins when the performer commits to change. Brian was a pleasure to work with from that point forward. He was curious to learn. He would write a page of notes at each meeting. He would not take my advice – he was too intelligent for that – instead he would take my suggestions and customize them.

In that second meeting I asked a simple question, 'When do you play at your best?'

Brian talked for what seemed like an hour. It was a significant breakthrough – the moment when he seemed to open up his mind completely. He spoke in minute detail about how he worked on his 'game knowledge' in advance of a match. This is his understanding of the tactics, the defensive set-up, how the opposition will play. It was very important to him to get that work done early in the week. He spoke about eating and hydrating very well all week, about training well and with great focus, working on the little extras during the days after training, chilling out and switching off. And then, when the match comes around, absolutely backing himself, trusting his judgement, trusting his instinct, seeing things before anyone else could.

This conversation made it easy to formulate a plan. The plan combined energy management with mental training, as well as aspects of Brian's role as a leader. Brian was amazing at executing the plan, and he was exceptional at delivering the big performance when his team needed it.

I had learned of a technique in America, from one of the leading performance coaches in the world. He compiled show-reels of tennis players' best moments and got them to watch these, over and over again. This is something I prepared for Brian – gathering footage of his best moments and using the highlights reel to reinforce the positives and boost his confidence. There was nothing particularly sophisticated about it, but Brian liked simple and effective ideas.

Confidence is like a muscle. The more you work it, the stronger it gets. The opposite is also true. The highlights reel is a sort of confidence résumé, a showcase of all the things that are great about you.

CONFIDENCE IS LIKE A MUSCLE. THE MORE YOU WORK IT, THE STRONGER IT GETS.

Obviously, most of us don't have our outstanding moments captured on film. But it's still an exercise you can replicate. Use pen and paper or a note-taking app on your phone. Make a list of all the great things you've done in your life, things that make you confident when you reflect on them.

'I worked hard and got a degree while studying at night.'

'I made a really good speech in front of a hundred people.'

'I raised a wonderful kid as a single parent.'

'I rebuilt my life after a divorce.'

Ahead of any big performance, any big challenge, keep your list with you. Read through it whenever you get a moment. It's a powerful way of programming yourself for greater confidence.

There was another breakthrough moment in that second session I had with Brian – possibly one of the biggest breakthrough moments I have ever experienced in working with top performers. I had asked Brian what he felt he was the best at on the team, and what were the aspects of his game that he needed to develop.

He was really relaxed and very open. Towards the end of the conversation he stopped talking, sat back in his chair, put his hands behind his head and said, 'I need to stick to my strengths.' And that's exactly what he did.

For the following five years it could be argued that Brian was consistently one of the top rugby players in the world. Playing to your greatest strengths sounds very logical and easy to do. But committing to doing it and working on it relentlessly, as Brian did, is very rare.

In previous chapters I talked about Martin Seligman's 'What's Working Well' exercise and the studies that demonstrate how it contributes to well-being. Positive psychology has given us another exercise that has also been found to boost well-being significantly – the 'Signature Strengths' exercise. The exercise couldn't be simpler – determine exactly what your signature strengths are, and then use one or more of those strengths in a new way every day. Doing this has been shown to increase happiness scores and lower depression scores in a range of tests.

So not only does playing to your strengths improve your performance, it also makes you feel better.

14

THE POWER OF VISUALIZATION

To the rational mind, much of the visualization work we have talked about in the previous chapters sounds slightly silly. How can merely thinking about something – which is what simulation and visualization are, when you get right down to it – actually bring about change?

This is exactly the question that exercise physiologist Guang Yue of the Cleveland Clinic Foundation in Ohio asked himself, back in 2001, before embarking on a series of experiments to see if visualization could be seen to work in laboratory conditions.

In the research, reported that year in the *New Scientist*, researchers at the foundation asked ten volunteers to imagine flexing their biceps as hard as possible in training sessions five times a week. These were monitored sessions, during which the subjects were wired up to record what was happening in their brains during visualization. The research team also monitored the electrical impulses in the motor neurons of the arm muscles, to make sure that the volunteers were not flexing their biceps unwittingly.

What they found after a few weeks was that the volunteers who merely thought about exercise saw a 13.5% increase in strength. Moreover, they held on to that strength for three months after the training stopped. (And no, the researchers did not include couch potatoes in their study – but I'm fairly confident this isn't effective if you never exercise in the first place!) A control group, which did not complete the visualizations, showed no increase in strength.

Gaining the psychological edge

I've been using visualization to prepare for performance since I was fourteen years old. It was particularly successful in one of the recurring challenges of my footballing career. Marking Peter Canavan.

My job for Armagh was always the same. I was never the player to score 2-4, that was never my skill set. But I was able to stop the guy who was able to score 2-4. That was my job. I was always put on their best forward with strict instructions. *Don't let him score.*

Peter Canavan was one of the best forwards of his generation: fast, elusive, deadly accurate. My preparation ahead of a match against Peter was very, very comprehensive, and it began long before the next Armagh–Tyrone fixture was even scheduled.

First, I'd go watch him play for his club, Errigal Ciarán, or for Tyrone.

Second, I'd watch video footage of him. Peter did me a great favour by bringing out an instructional video for kids on how to play the game. I used to watch that, over and over, studying his moves and how he did what he did, to the point where when I dreamed, all I could see was Canavan twisting and turning and trying to slide past me.

Next, I recruited my little brother Patrick, who grew up during those Armagh glory days. Patrick adored Canavan and he'd watch that video with me time after time. Patrick was also a magic footballer – exceptionally skilful – and after we'd watched the video for the fiftieth time, I'd get him out on the pitch at home.

'Patrick, solo at me,' I'd say.

You can't hit your little brother a shoulder, but you can't hit Peter Canavan either. He's smaller and lighter than me. You hit him, he's going to go down and you're going to end up giving away a free at the very least. So I'd try to strip the ball off Patrick without touching him.

And the last thing: lying in bed at night, I would go into my visualizations. First, I would relax my mind. Then my body, by doing a progressive muscular relaxation exercise.

You do that by working through every muscle group, from your calf muscles to your quads to your hamstrings to your glutes to your abdominal muscles to your chest muscles to your shoulder muscles. Right through the body and up to your forehead. Tensing and inhaling, relaxing and exhaling.

Then I'd start to picture it. Marking Canavan. Not just picture it. Hear it, see it, smell it, feel it. It was always a very specific scenario – whether it was a league game, or an All-Ireland semi-final, or an All-Ireland final.

I would visualize what would happen when the first ball came in. Say it came in high – Canavan, despite his size, was brilliant in the air – I'd visualize what I'd do, how I might even let him catch the ball, but when he came down I'd be like a basketball player, shepherding him towards the sideline. I would make sure that he never got an inch of space, because all he needed was an inch of space to score.

I'd go through the scenarios:

If he got the ball in front of goal, how was I going to respond?

If he got the ball away out on the wing, how would I respond?

Canavan would always get tired after maybe fifteen minutes of play and would take a couple of minutes to recuperate. Lying in bed, I would hear his familiar wheeze, and I would visualize myself, during those few minutes when he was weak, stepping up my game, stepping up my aggression. I would feed off his weakness and become stronger. When those couple of minutes came, I would always let him know I was there, stronger than ever, better than ever, more ready for him than ever.

And it worked.

Peter Canavan never scored from play in any game in which I marked him.

> **PETER CANAVAN NEVER SCORED FROM PLAY IN ANY GAME IN WHICH I MARKED HIM.**

I was on the All Stars trip to the States in 2003, as was Peter. We were chatting in a bar in San Diego. Despite our on-pitch rivalry, we got on fine off the pitch.

Anyway, another of the Tyrone players came over and said, 'Peter, I can't believe you're talking to Enda McNulty. Sure, he wrecked your Achilles.' (I had fallen on Peter going for a ball earlier that year, which resulted in an Achilles injury.) Your man went on, 'Sure, the only reason Enda can mark you is that he is dirty and constantly fouls you.'

Peter then said something that I will never forget. It gave me an insight into how I'd gained a major psychological edge over one of the greatest footballers in a generation.

'In fairness, no,' he said. 'Enda didn't try to injure me. He never had to.'

Picturing success

I met David Gillick in a gym in Dublin, shortly after he had won gold in the 400 metres at the European Athletics Indoor Championships, in 2005, and we chatted for a bit.

I said, 'Listen, if you ever want some help with your mental toughness, I'd be happy to give you some advice.'

He said, 'Yeah, I'd love to meet up. We'll have to do that.'

I didn't hear from David again. I know now that I should have followed up. But at the time, I hadn't been in the business long enough to understand that.

About a year or eighteen months later, I ran into him in a bar in Dundrum. I'd just started the company, with no income, no office, no safe capital. I was sleeping on a mattress that I had got for nothing at a fire sale. The banks and the business advisers had all laughed at me. So I was hungry for work.

Since I had last met him, I knew that things weren't going so well for David either. He was in a performance slump and struggling to regain his form. We chatted and then arranged to meet the following day.

We met in an Italian restaurant in Dundrum and talked for about ninety minutes. He was at a crossroads, trying to decide whether to continue to train in Ireland or move to the next level and relocate to the UK, where there were coaches and facilities that were much better than anything we had at the time.

The restaurant had paper tablecloths – brown on one side, white on the other. As we talked, I flipped mine over and started to write.

I asked him, 'Where do you want to go? What do you want to do with your career?'

We batted this back and forth for a while before he told me that he wanted to become one of the top athletes in the world.

'So what does that mean? The top thirty, forty, fifty?'

At this stage he was ranked sixty-seventh in the world.

He said, 'I want to get into the top ten.'

'OK, great. So what sort of times do you want to run?'

'I want to run sub 45 seconds in the 400 metres.'

'OK, how many Irish athletes have ever done that?'

'None.'

'Oh, you're going to be the first Irish fella that does this?'

'That's it.'

On the back of that tablecloth, we started to work out a plan. We drew out a pyramid of success, a concept developed by the US basketball coach John Wooden (I talked about his definition of success in Chapter 9, 'Bouncing back'). It was incredibly detailed. Nothing was left out. We went through everything, from mental toughness to improving his nutrition, to Pilates, meditation, morning rituals, managing the media, his recovery, time spent with family, his technical running skills, his coaching. Block by block it all went in, and at the top we had the goal.

Running the 400 metres in under 45 seconds, and breaking into the top ten.

Not long after we began working together, David took the plunge and decided to move to the UK. The first big challenge he faced after his move was the European Athletics Indoor Championships in Birmingham, where he would be going in as defending champion.

David recalls:

'That added a bit of extra pressure to the whole thing. I'd relocated to England a month beforehand, so that added some expectation. I was worried I was going to false start, I was worried I'd run flat. I was imagining what people would think and say: "Jesus, David's made a mistake by going to England, he's gone backwards." And I was thinking about my funding too. Would I be able to hold on to my grant? My sponsors? All that worry boiled down to this: "What if I make a show of myself?"'

'ALL MY WORRY BOILED DOWN TO THIS: "WHAT IF I MAKE A SHOW OF MYSELF?"' DAVID GILLICK

I got David to write down his doubts, every one of them, big and small. As he did, I picked them up, read them out, and both of us laughed at them.

'Actually putting them down on paper, writing them down, helped me to realize just how stupid they were. That was a real calming influence. And then Enda got me to burn them all in the grate. And I did, and it felt good.'

A few weeks out from the big race in Birmingham we were in my flat in Ranelagh and I was guiding him through meditation and breathing.

Then I said, 'Right, get up. We're going to do some visualization.'

David opened one eye. 'We're what?'

'Stand up,' I said.

He stood up slowly.

'Right, where are you in the race?'

'Ah . . . I've just come out of the blocks.'

'But why are you standing up straight? You wouldn't be like that on the track.'

'Oh, right.'

So David sort of bent over and went into a kind of starting stance. Talk about half-hearted! I could tell he thought it was daft.

But I persisted. I began to talk him through it, getting him to do exactly what my father had done when he set out to recreate the experience of boarding a plane back in our house in Armagh. We talked about the sights and smells of the arena, the feel of the track underfoot, the temperature, the feel of the air, the sounds of the crowd, and so on.

As we conjured up all of these sensory details, my flat melted away and in its place we stood on the track in the National Indoor Arena in Birmingham.

Again, repetition was key. Time and again in the weeks leading up to that race, we did the same thing. And with each repetition, it became easier to do, so that within a couple of weeks David could summon up the venue and everything in it with accuracy and ease.

I showed him a motivational video built around the idea that at 211°F water is hot, but at 212°F, it turns into steam, and steam can power locomotives. One degree is the difference between hot water and an unstoppable force. The idea is that if you can go one degree further, just a single degree, it can make all the difference. That idea really appealed to David, and it would turn out to be pivotal in what happened later.

'I used to write 212 on my hand. I was going down training and other people would be looking, going, "What's 212 mean?" And I'd just be like, "Ah, it's a room I have to go to later on for, you know, a lecture." Because I didn't want to have to go into a big spiel about it.'

That '212' evolved into a little circle on his hand, then just a dot. That would be enough. Things like that helped to remind him what it was all about.

'I wanted to run world-class times. I wanted to run the 400 metres in 45 seconds. That was my purpose, my passion. That's why I was there. I needed reminding of that, because I'd made a decision to leave all my friends, my family, my girlfriend. Some days I just wanted to go home, I missed home, I missed my friends. I'd be asking myself, "What am I doing over here? I don't know anyone. Is it going to pay off?" And just looking down at that dot on my hand triggered everything it symbolized. That helped an awful lot.'

At the race itself, David went into a sort of cocoon. He had a well-established pre-race routine that never varied, that helped him get into exactly the right frame of mind for the challenge ahead.

'Then, on the blocks, I said to myself, "Right, dynamite is lit." I blessed myself, said my prayer and told myself, "I'm going to run well." And when the gun went off, the dynamite exploded.'

The race itself was very, very close. He won it 'on the dip', by one tenth of a second – that one degree he had written on his hand.

'I can remember when I dipped, I looked down at the line and I realized I'd won, and it felt as if I had already been there. Such a powerful sense of déjà vu. That was because I had visualized it so many times in the weeks prior to it. I had visualized everything: the sound of the crowd, the smell of the gun, the feel of the track, even my celebration at the end. I'd seen it all before. I had visualized everything.'

It was, he says, a very surreal experience. And though I've been doing it a long time, I can understand that sense of strangeness when visualization works. There is something surreal about finally meeting the reality you've been simulating for so long.

David still has the tablecloth from the restaurant where we worked out his plan that day. And in 2009, he achieved his goal. He ran the 400 metres in 44.77 seconds, setting a new Irish record that still hasn't been beaten.

By the end of that year, he was ranked fifth in the world.

MENTAL STRENGTH – TAKE ACTION NOW!

1. *Write down a list of your biggest strengths in a journal.* Really reflect on what you are strongest at. Make sure you know your biggest strengths off by heart.

2. *Spend fifteen minutes each day mentally rehearsing how you want to perform.* Do this before your next big performance. Try to do it just before you drift off to sleep.

3. *Write out your confidence résumé.* Compile a list of all the things you have done in your career/life that give you confidence. Add to this constantly and try to read it once a day.

4. *Practise using positive affirmations.* The next time you exercise or train, see the session as an opportunity to train mentally as well as physically. Keep repeating positive statements in your head, over and over, as you train. Combine it with listening to your favourite music. Monitor how confident and strong you feel before and after.

5. *Pick a real-life situation and devise a mental rehearsal script.* Use any source you can to fine-tune your simulation, making it as close to the real thing as possible. Repeat the visualization ten times a day, fourteen days in a row.

FLOW

15

GETTING IN THE ZONE

Yes, preparation is everything. If you don't do the work, if you don't set out to control everything that can be controlled, you will not perform to your potential. But when it comes to the performance itself, unfortunately – even with all the best preparation in the world – it's not enough.

Back in the early days with Armagh, I used to tape up my wrists, then write different cue words on each strip of tape. I might have 'First step quickness' on one. I might have 'Attack aggressively' on another, something like 'Be confident' on a third, 'Anticipate well' on a fourth . . . there could be a dozen of these little messages, running halfway up my forearm.

It was too much. I was complicating my mental approach.

I was cluttering up my mind instead of leaving myself free to just play, to get into the zone. Ideally, when you perform you want to empty your mind. But I was thinking too much. Analysing too much. Interpreting too much. Worrying too much. Thinking about the future too much. Reflecting on the past too much. Dissecting the performance too much.

The other day I was listening to a tenor talking about performing. He said that the more he thought about vocal
projection, the more difficult it became to achieve. I've
worked with a lot of elite golfers, and it's the same thing.
Think too much about missing the cut, or about how you
could win or lose the Masters on the back of the next drive,
and you're lost.

So many of us get in our own way and sabotage our own
performance.

The more you dissect things, the more you scrutinize each
movement, while you are performing, the more the mental
handbrake goes on. Mental training and performance coaching ultimately aim to free you up, so you can go and perform
to your full potential.

Ahead of any big performance, spend the early part of
the week mentally training, using some of the ideas I
described in the previous section. Ideally, have all the mental
and physical preparation locked in by midweek. Then relax.
Switch off all the analytics and the dissections and the apprais-
als. Power it all down. Then go play. The time for thought is
over.

The ground-breaking research here was carried out by
the Hungarian psychologist Mihály Csíkszentmihályi, back
in the 1970s, while running the University of Chicago's psychology department. Csíkszentmihályi's proposition, borne
out by his research, was that human beings are happiest
when they are so completely absorbed in something that
the rest of the world falls away. Then they are in a state of
'flow'.

It might be a game of tennis, making a speech, herding
sheep, selling a product, holding a conversation with a friend.
It might be listening to a wonderful piece of music or painting

a picture. The flow state happens when you are so fully engrossed in what you're doing that nothing else matters. You are relaxed and engaged with the now, rather than focusing on what happened before, or what's going to happen later. You're not focused on an outcome, nor on being the best. You are totally unselfconscious, and effortlessly inhabit the moment. You are so completely absorbed that your troubles recede into the background.

> **THE FLOW STATE HAPPENS WHEN YOU ARE SO FULLY ENGROSSED IN WHAT YOU'RE DOING THAT NOTHING ELSE MATTERS.**

In the flow state, your whole being is connected to whatever you are doing. You have a sense of unity with the process. You are at one with the piano, the pen, the microphone, the paintbrush, the chisel, the trowel. You are winning twenty-one breaking balls, you are writing more in a sitting than in the previous month, you are lost in the music or the dance or the book. You don't get hungry or thirsty. You lose track of time.

Stop overthinking

When I look back on my footballing life I think that, despite the fact that I won a lot, I achieved maybe 30% of my potential. Having worked with a lot of elite athletes, I now know that I made a lot of mistakes in regard to my mental preparation.

I trained way too hard at the wrong time and didn't rest enough. It's telling that when I was first invited on to the Armagh panel, I couldn't go to the first training sessions because I had two hernias brought on by over-training.

Also, I was obsessively focused on being successful. Instead of just relaxing and playing football, I was hamstrung by wanting to win too much, by wanting to fulfil my role perfectly. That actually held me back.

It comes down to this – sometimes, you've got to try softer, not harder.

I wish I had known that sooner.

I met an old sage many years ago who used that phrase when I was describing how I prepared and practised. He listened, smiled and gently said, 'Enda, try softer.' It was great advice, probably the best advice I ever received. Unfortunately, my football career was over by the time I realized it. But I hope it's not too late for you.

If there is one person I could say has managed to achieve the flow state more readily and effectively than anyone else I've worked with, it's the Kerry footballer Paul Galvin.

I had misgivings about working with Paul. I was still playing for Armagh when we first met, in 2009, and Kerry was the old enemy. But after Armagh got knocked out, and with Kerry still in contention, I met with Paul and we talked about his game.

He had nearly quit after getting sent off in the Munster final replay against Cork. And despite the fact that he still had loads to give, he was feeling pretty negative about things. One thing was very clear – he was so stressed and wound up going into matches that his emotions frequently got the better of him.

I told him, 'You're far too tense, far too hyped up. You're far too aggressive. You're using your energy like a boxer, in trading blows. No need for that. You need to use your energy to make intelligent runs, score points, win breaking balls. Not in the combustion of the one-on-ones.'

It was clear to me that he was over-thinking the games themselves. In the run-up to a big match, he thought about nothing else. He needed to switch off, to find distractions outside football.

The very idea appalled him. Find distractions? From football? Stop thinking about football?

But like all high achievers, all great leaders, he was open to learning, to trying a new way. So he went off and found new hobbies, other things to occupy his mind. He developed his interests in music and fashion.

Now, running on to the pitch, his mind was free and uncluttered. He was totally relaxed. Watching him then on the pitch in the flow state was a complete joy. How chilled he was, how much in the moment he was.

It was impressive how, in a short amount of time, he'd elevated himself mentally and emotionally to a completely different place. Possibly the most effectively I'd ever seen anybody do it. He was electric for the rest of 2009, and thoroughly deserved his Footballer of the Year award.

Breathe

Before you can enter the flow state and perform at your best, you need to empty your mind. Not an easy thing to do.

Psychologists have researched how many thoughts humans have per day. Estimates vary, but it's anything between 15,000 and 60,000 thoughts a day. Our minds are cluttered with a dozen different thoughts, fifteen different priorities, twenty different anxieties. But flow does not occur when the mind is overactive.

How can you try to get into the flow state?

Try this first. Focus on the body.

I mentioned progressive muscle relaxation in Chapter 14, 'The power of visualization'. It's something I learned to do while still a teenager. It means tensing and relaxing every muscle in your body in sequence. Begin with the muscles in the bottom of your feet. Scrunch up your feet as hard as you can, as if you're trying to pick up a sheaf of paper with your toes. Do that for ten seconds, taking a deep breath in as you do so, then relax the muscles and exhale. Move to your calves and do the same thing. Take a deep breath in and as you're breathing in, tense your muscles as tightly as you can, then exhale and relax. Keep going, using the same pattern, right up to your forehead, then back down your body again.

This process focuses the mind on the body, and helps to empty the mind.

Meditation is another wonderful way of clearing the mind and preparing for the moment when all of the preparations you've done can come together, when you can freely, thoughtlessly slip into the zone and simply perform.

Here are a few ideas to add to your meditation playlist.

1. Focus on your breathing for ten counts. Deep breath in, deep breath out.
2. Focus on your exhalation in particular. Again for ten counts. Almost observe your exhalation.
3. Focus on your *hara*, as you breathe. It lies one inch below your navel. Ten counts, breathing in, breathing out.
4. Super slow exhalation. Make the exhalation three times longer than normal.
5. Ten short, fast inhalations through your nose, then ten short, fast exhalations out through your nose.

6. Close your left nostril and breathe in and out through your right for ten breaths. Then close your right nostril and repeat.

7. Whisper this mantra as you breathe in: 'I shall breathe in.' And this as you breathe out: 'I shall breathe out.' Repeat five times.

8. Whisper this mantra as you breathe in: 'I shall breathe in calm.' And this as you breathe out: 'I shall breathe out stress.'

Now, let's focus on getting the body into peak state.

If I'm waiting to go on stage, I start to get my body activated, get it energized – moving all the muscle groups, slapping myself up and down my arms, my legs, my torso.

Think of yourself as a human performance system. How you perform in any context doesn't just depend on what happens from the neck up. You are your whole body, from the tips of your toes to the top of your head. Before you go into the meeting – or the interview, or whatever it is – do some light stretches. Wake the body up, prepare it for the chal-

YOU ARE YOUR WHOLE BODY, FROM THE TIPS OF YOUR TOES TO THE TOP OF YOUR HEAD.

lenge to come. You want to get that entire performance system operating. Get yourself physically, mentally and emotionally warmed up.

Now, remind yourself of your best ever performance. Remind yourself of that moment when you slipped into the zone and became your best self.

When I think of my best ever performance it's in the All-Ireland semi-final against Dublin, in 2002 (a career-defining event I referred to in my opening Preface). I remember

Croke Park seething, heaving, rattling. The noise poured down from the stands. I was sick with nerves. My legs were like jelly walking in the parade. I thought, *I can't do this*. I was going to tell the manager, Joe Kernan, that I'd pulled a hamstring, that I couldn't play.

By then I'd put a lot of work into managing my mind, and as we walked around Croke Park and the band played and the crowd roared, I began to shift my mental state. Looking around, taking it all in, my eye fell on an advertisement for Guinness. G for Guinness . . . G for 'great mental toughness'. Next, I saw an AIB hoarding. A for 'acceleration', 'as good as anybody on the pitch'. From that moment on, I decided to shift my mental state. I looked around and found visual cues to reconnect me with the reasons why I was there, with all that was great about my game. Instead of carrying around a scribbled cacophony of messages on my arms, I was taking what I needed from where I was and then moving on.

Then came the anthem, and as it played I made another decision: I would be tall, strong, ready for anything. I rose into my peak state. After the anthem, I remember jumping up and down on my toes, injecting good energy into my body. I remember feeling that energy coursing through my veins.

Then I made a third decision. A final commitment. *Go for it*. I nodded to myself. *Go for it*.

The referee blew the whistle, threw in the ball. One of the Dublin midfielders caught it and sent it spinning towards me and Alan Brogan, who I was marking. I moved. I remember the ball came in at a nice height, I was behind Brogan, I jumped, got a fist to it, shouldered Brogan, collected the ball, soloed it, hand passed . . . And I was in. I was there, in the flow. Time stopped. There was just the match and me. I was in control. My communications were perfect, and I was on top of every situation. I had the energy for 300 matches.

It was as if, when the whistle blew for half-time, I was woken out of a trance. It was the best half-hour's football I had ever played.

Now, when I'm about to stand up in front of an auditorium full of people, that half-hour of pure football is what I remind myself of and try to connect with. This was when the work I had done over the previous ten years – the preparation, the sacrifice, the pain and ambition – all flowed together, and my thinking mind shut down and I just played.

Remembering this gets me to a good place, gets me confident. As I'm about to launch into a new performance, this past experience is preparing me. I'm projecting earlier success on to the future, and seeing the future in the light of that success.

So now, having got yourself warmed up and mentally primed, you are ready – physically, mentally, emotionally. You stand up, you move, you open the door, you begin.

You step into flow.

In flow, you've cleared your mind of all distractions. You don't think about the outcome. The outcome is irrelevant. You're focused entirely on the process. The only thing on your mind is the here and now – whether it's the game, or the song, or the pen in your hand, or the people in front of you.

Time stops, and you're wholly immersed in what you're doing.

Just enjoy it

That experience of total absorption and connection with what I was doing in the 2002 semi-final gave me an experience of flow that will live with me for the rest of my life. I now love inspiring and educating people all over the world about how to find their flow.

In 2000, shortly before the All-Ireland semi-final against Kerry, I was at Dessie Ryan's daughter's wedding. Though I was at the wedding in body, my mind was focused on the match and nothing else. The dancing, the food, the craic, it all passed me by.

Dessie being Dessie, there was a lot of footballing royalty at the wedding, including Eamonn Coleman, the great Derry footballer and manager.

I knew I was going to be marking Mike Frank Russell in the match, and all I could think of when I met Eamonn was to ask his advice.

'What do you think, Eamonn? Should I mark him from the inside or the outside? What would you do?'

I'll never forget Eamonn's broad smile, the big blue eyes shining.

'Enda,' he said, 'just enjoy it.'

'Yeah, but Eamonn, you know the way he twists and turns, those dummies of his, you know. What'll I do about those?'

Again, his reply was, 'Just enjoy it.'

I would not let it go. I asked him a third time, and again he shook his head.

'Enda,' he said, 'just get out there and enjoy it.'

Did I do that?

No, I did not.

I over-trained and over-thought and went in there too wound up, unable to play. As I said earlier, I hadn't prepared properly to deal with a heaving, seething Croke Park.

We were outgunned and outmanoeuvred. Kerry beat us in extra time in the replay.

Three times Eamonn Coleman gave me one of the most valuable pieces of advice I would ever get, but I just wasn't yet in a place where I could take it in.

There was probably too much emphasis on football in my life. I let it consume too much of me. I wish I'd done something different, I wish I'd taken a year out and travelled around the world.

Relationships I had – with my friends, my family, my girl-friends – they all suffered. There were a lot of weddings I didn't go to, a lot of family occasions I missed, a lot of christenings and engagement parties that I turned down.

Mine was the sort of commitment that gives commitment a bad name:

'Sorry I can't go, I have Armagh training.'

'Sorry I can't go, I'm training with Queen's.'

'Sorry I can't go, I'm on a training weekend.'

'Sorry I can't go to your wedding, we have a training camp in Spain that week.'

I remember phoning up one of the first Armagh coaches I played under and telling him that I couldn't go training that night because my best friend's dad had died and I had to go to the wake.

'Enda,' he said, 'you don't miss Armagh training for a wake. If you're not at training, you're not on the squad.'

I still got to the wake, but it was at midnight after driving for two hours. Great life lesson.

In all the years I played, I didn't get into the flow state often enough. I achieved it from time to time, but not regularly enough. And now I look back, I realize why – I tried too hard. I prepped too much and didn't recover well enough. I tried to cram too much in. I analysed too much. I was too worried about consequences, about outcomes.

When I was playing with Armagh, I was fitting in an hour and a half of mental preparation four times a week. Crazy stuff. And then there were meetings with my sports psychologist, goal-setting sessions, review sessions – way too much thinking and mental preparation.

Now we keep things very simple for the athletes and performers we work with. The mental training programmes last no longer than twenty minutes, five times a week. The best performers focus and practise as intensely during this period as they would do on the training pitch, or as a dancer would do in a group practice session.

I wish I had enjoyed my sport more. That is a big regret, but I use that regret as a source of energy so I can inspire others to enjoy their performance more. These days, I try to make sure that all our coaching sessions start with fun and end with fun. My colleagues will start meetings with positives and end with positives.

I WISH I HAD ENJOYED MY SPORT MORE.

At some of our team meetings some of my colleagues will do a fun confidence-boosting exercise called 'Wall of Belief'. It's a simple exercise where we each post up the things we've done that give us more belief and confidence in ourselves.

What are our strengths?

What are our big successes?

Our small successes?

What are our small wins?

What are the big positives?

Reading Eckhart Tolle's *The Power of Now* had a big impact on me. It helped me to realize the danger of constantly chasing your dreams – chasing another client, or another contract, or another business venture . . . or another All-Ireland, as I did for ten years. You have to realize that the only place you can be happy is now.

Fifteen years of professional experience has proved to me that most of us spend too much of our lives in the future or the past.

Try doing this simple exercise to help you reconnect with the now.

Focus on your breath. Your breath is your bridge to the moment. By focusing on your breath, you're centring yourself in the now. You can't breathe in the past, you can't breathe in the future.

The only place you can ever breathe is in the now.

16

WHEN DREAMS COME TRUE

Having talked about the darker side of chasing your dreams, let me bring this book to its conclusion by sharing the joy of having a dream come true, in the hope that it will encourage you to figure out your own dreams and commit to making them happen.

Because while there are always regrets and mistakes and wrong turnings, some things we do right. Some things come good and are totally and completely worth the sacrifice.

On 22 September 2002, I woke up in my hotel room and shuffled out to the bathroom. As I opened the door, the light caught something on the floor, just inside the room. An envelope. I went over, picked it up, tore open the top and pulled out a piece of paper. A letter. I scanned it to the bottom and saw the scrawl.

Muhammad Ali.

I ran my thumb over the signature – it was real, it was really him.

The letter was all about the challenge that lay before us on this day, about chasing your dreams and stepping up to your potential.

That was some way to start the day.

Everyone got one of these letters. Slipped under the door in the dead of night by Hugh Campbell, Armagh's mental toughness coach. Somehow or other – and in the excitement of the day I never found out how – Hugh had got Muhammad Ali to sign letters to a team of footballers in Ireland.

The nerves, the nerves, the nerves.

Going down the corridor to the dining room for breakfast, I felt like my legs were going to pop. Then later, making our way downstairs, the lobby of the hotel was packed with Armagh supporters. From the top of the stairs, all we could see were these swarms of orange and white. There were roars and applause as we trooped down the stairs and made our way out through the fans – I felt like we were sheep making our way through a wood.

The anxiety deepened, the sense of nervous anticipation grew.

I went straight to the back of the bus, the same seat I always took, right-hand side at the very back, in beside the same guys: Paul McGrane, my brother Justin, Steven McDonnell, Kieran McGeeney, Paddy McKeever and Aidan O'Rourke. That was the back-seat formation, and it never varied.

Garda escort down the N7, on to the M50, and into town.

Everywhere we turned, our eyes picked out the orange and white, the flags on the cars alongside the bus. Then, the closer we got to the stadium, the people on the street – kids, dads, mums, old men, old women – when they spotted the bus, they would turn in response to a shout or a tap on the shoulder and their eyes would light up and they would clap and shout. The closer we got, the thicker the crowds. They'd slap the sides of the coach.

The anxiety deepened, and with it came a creeping sense of inadequacy.

No matter how much we'd trained, or what we'd done, I felt unprepared. I felt like everything was new and unfamiliar, that there was no way we – I, any of us – were up for the enormity of the challenge that lay ahead. This was a pivotal moment in my life – this dawning realization that we hadn't done enough mental preparation. (This moment, perhaps more than any other, has shaped my business and explains why I have attempted to forge mental toughness in the sportspeople, business executives, artists and other clients I have worked with in my company.)

Benny Tierney made a joke – Benny was always making jokes – and that eased the tension a bit. For a while, at least. Then getting off the bus – *bang!* The TV cameras right in our faces.

Again, I wasn't prepared for that. I had no idea they'd be there. That was a shock, and it ramped up the tension and the sense of what was at stake.

In the dressing rooms, again, I craved the familiar. Same seat beside the same guy. I went through the same mental and physical routine, as everybody did. Whether it was checking studs, taping ankles and wrists, left ankle, right ankle, left wrist, right wrist. Then into the warm-up room, kicking a ball, in socks first, left foot, right foot, against the wall. Then down on the floor, gentle stretching. Then into team warm-ups.

The tension in the room.

The nerves, the nerves, the nerves.

There was no talking, a lot of balls being dropped. Then the talk picked up, the noise picked up. And now accuracy improved, I started to control my breathing. The nerves seemed to be coming under control. But then running out on to the pitch. Back they came.

I always felt the nerves in my legs. I thought my legs were going to pop, my hamstrings felt like they were going to burst. The thing was to try to cover as much ground as possible before going back in for the photograph.

Get to feel it all, see it all.

Then the photograph. There were four men from our club: Kieran McGeeney (the captain), Benny Tierney, Justin and me. I remember the pride, but especially the closeness of it. We had our arms around each other. It was almost intimate.

> **I THOUGHT MY LEGS WERE GOING TO POP, MY HAMSTRINGS FELT LIKE THEY WERE GOING TO BURST.**

Then we pulled apart.

Paul McGrane called what he always called: 'First whistle!'

It meant this: *We're going to go at this, from the first whistle to the last.*

The first half?

In the first half the fullback line got annihilated. We were playing one of the greatest full forward lines, possibly ever – Dara Ó Cinnéide, Colm Cooper and Mike Frank Russell. I started out marking Mike Frank, then I got switched to Cooper, but I was at sea.

Totally at sea.

There were acres of space in front of the full forward line, and the quality of ball being played into the three forwards was inch-perfect.

And I had made a major error of judgement in my footwear. Someone had advised me that I should be wearing a particular brand of studs and, stupidly, I had listened. And

COMMIT!

now I was slipping around like the pitch was a skating rink. In the semi-final I'd had the game of my life against the Dubs and I hadn't slipped. But I'd still gone ahead and changed my boots. Now it looked as though that foolish decision was going to cost us an All-Ireland.

This I put down to lack of experience. I should have known better. A more experienced player wouldn't have changed.

While I was skidding around Croke Park, and Mike Frank and Colm Cooper were having a field day, the most import-ant moment of my footballing life was about to happen. Even now, Armagh people talk to me about this moment. For anybody who was at that match, this is one of the things they remember.

It's halfway through the first half and we're getting roasted.

Benny Tierney runs out and he roars at me, 'Enda, you're going to have to get in front!'

Now, typically, a corner back plays behind the forward; you stay goal-side of him so that if he wins the ball and turns, you are there to stop him. The disadvantage, of course, is that you're surrendering possession of the ball, plus you have to second-guess what he's going to do.

On this particular day, the ball was coming in so fast and so furious and so incredibly accurately that we kept getting caught. So Benny tells me to get in front. Cut the supply off.

Sixty seconds after he said that, a ball came in. Another perfect ball pinged in, and it had Cooper's name all over it.

I thought to myself, *I'm going to have to go for broke here, or this is over anyway*. I remember almost nodding to myself, taking that decision. Committing to it. *Just go for it, whatever the hell it takes. You have to get something out of this.*

224

In came the ball, I burst forward and jumped. And as I did, I had a flashback. Time slowed down and it was eight years earlier . . .

I am seventeen years old. 1994. Ulster Minor Final. I go for a ball in the air. As a fullback, as a corner back, this is what you're always doing – you're always taking rapid-fire decisions. Are you going to go, or are you going to hold back and mind the house? And the way it works is, if you get the ball, you're a hero. If you don't, you're a fool. And often, the margin – the dividing line between heroism and idiocy – is wafer thin. This time, I decide to go for it. So I jump. I stretch out my hand and watch the ball sail over my head in slow motion. It is in the back of the net almost before I hit the ground. And I'm the fool.

Now here I was, jumping again, gambling again.

Here I was, going for the same ball, this time in front of 85,000 people in the biggest game of my life.

I was about to do the stupidest thing a corner back can do.

Once again, I could see that ball about to go over my head – this time into the grateful arms of Colm Cooper, one of the greatest finishers the game has ever seen.

Oh shit, oh shit.

I reached for the ball.

I felt myself hanging in the air, way off the ground.

And then I felt it. The ball.

The very tip of my outstretched finger had got a touch of the ball.

As I came down, I knew it was enough. I knew it was going to bounce in front of me.

Somewhere behind me, Cooper was stranded.

The ball bounced, I claimed it and gave it off.

Now, if I talk to anyone about that game, that's what they remember about my performance. We were down four or five points when that ball came in. If it wasn't for the miracle of that moment, it would have been seven or eight. There would have been no coming back from that, we would have been dead and buried.

So many times, people have said to me, 'Enda, if you hadn't have got that ball, it was curtains.'

Half-time.

I couldn't get off the pitch fast enough. I needed to change my boots.

We were four points down, but we hadn't played well. We'd done OK in pockets – for a few minutes at the start and at the end of the half.

Now, Joe came in. Big Joe Kernan, the Armagh manager.

To his eternal credit, he had planned for a situation such as this. He produced the plaque he had received as a member of the losing team in 1977, when Armagh was stuffed by Dublin in the final. It was black with a little gold medal on it.

He was standing almost in the shower room in the corner when he started talking.

IF WE LOST, HE TOLD US, FOR THE REST OF OUR LIVES WE WOULD BE REMEMBERED AS THE 'NEARLY' MEN.

If we lost, he told us, for the rest of our lives we would be remembered as the 'nearly' men. And we would always regret being losers. Not only for the rest of our lives in sport, but for the rest of our lives.

Full stop. We'd be remembered as the guys who got to an All-Ireland final and got beaten, just like he was.

'That's me. I'm only remembered as a guy on the team that got to the All-Ireland final and got stuffed by the Dubs. That'll be on my tombstone. What're you guys going to be? Are yiz going to be losers for the rest of your lives?

'What sorta men are yiz? Are yiz goin' to be losers like me? I'm a loser, for the rest of my life I'll be renowned as a loser. Well, I'm sick of being a loser!'

And with that he took his plaque – from where I was sitting, I couldn't see exactly what happened to it – and it sounded like he smashed it into smithereens. The rattle of the bits hitting the tiled floor echoed all around the shower room.

The effect was electrifying. In the space of a few minutes our mental state underwent a huge change. We had been hunched over, staring at the floor, the smell of missed opportunity thick in the air. Now we began to move. Our heads came back up, and we began to look at each other.

'He's right. C'mon, let's go and win this thing. We're playing terrible, we're not putting them under enough pressure. We know we can beat them . . .'

'We need to tackle as if our lives depended on it . . .'

'We need to hunt every breaking ball like dogs . . .'

'We need to dominate every one-to-one battle . . .'

Everyone in the crowd, the pundits at half-time, anyone who'd seen the first half – they had all decided we were stuffed. If you were to poll everyone in Croke Park at half-time, they would have said that it was Kerry's game.

But the fifteen Armagh players who ran out on to that pitch for the second half knew differently.

We made a collective decision that we would be winners for the rest of our lives, not losers, and that was all down to

Joe Kernan's little piece of psychological wizardry. Because of the fire he had lit in our bellies, it was us up there on the Hogan Stand after the final whistle, not Kerry.

More importantly, we had made a collective decision that we would be winners for the rest of our lives.

READING LIST

Maya Angelou, *I Know Why the Caged Bird Sings*, Virago, 1984

Mihály Csíkszentmihályi, *Flow: The Psychology of Happiness*, Rider, 2002

Carol Dweck, *Mindset*, Robinson, 2012

Tim Foster, *Four Men in a Boat*, Orion, 2004

Victor Frankl, *Man's Search for Meaning*, Rider, 2004

W. Timothy Gallwey, *The Inner Game of Tennis*, Pan, 1986

Malcolm Gladwell, *David & Goliath*, Penguin, 2014

Jack L. Groppel, *The Corporate Athlete: How to Achieve Maximal Performance in Business and Life*, John Wiley & Sons, 1999

Felicity Heathcote, *Peak Performance: Zen and the Sporting Zone*, Merlin Publishing, 1996

Napoleon Hill, *Think and Grow Rich*, Wilder Publications, 2007

Ryan Holiday, *The Obstacle is the Way*, Profile Books, 2015

Michael Johnson, *Gold Rush*, HarperSport, 2012

Michael Johnson, *Slaying the Dragon*, Piatkus Books, 1996

Michael Jordan, *Driven from Within*, Atria Books, 2006

John Kremer and Aidan Moran, *Sport: Practical Sport Psychology*, Routledge, 2013

Randy Pausch and Jeffrey Zaslow, *The Last Lecture*, Two Roads, 2010

James W. Pennebaker, *Opening Up: The Healing Power of Confiding in Others*, Avon Books, 1991

Tony Robbins, *Awaken the Giant Within*, Simon & Schuster UK, 2001

Ian Robertson, *The Winner Effect: How Power Affects your Brain*, Bloomsbury, 2012

Bob Rotella, *Your Fifteenth Club: The Inner Secret to Great Golf*, Simon & Schuster UK, 2009

Martin Seligman, *Flourish*, Nicholas Brealey, 2011

Ernest Shackleton, *South*, Penguin Classics, 2015

Robin Sharma, *The Monk Who Sold His Ferrari*, Harper Thorsons, 2015

Joe Simpson, *Touching the Void*, Vintage, 1998

Ekhart Tolle, *The Power of Now*, Yellow Kite, 2001

Brian Tracy, *Flight Plan*, Berrett-Koehler, 2009

John Wooden, Jay Carty, David Robinson, *Coach Wooden's Pyramid of Success*, Revell, 2009

ACKNOWLEDGEMENTS

John Hearne made this book possible. He burned the mid-night oil at his writer's table in Galway for almost two years. His stamina was massive the whole way through this process. John kept me focused and on track, no matter where I was in the world. He was patient, humble and incredibly helpful. Most importantly, he downloaded what was in my head like a master craftsman. John, you have been a class act, a great professional, and you have made writing the book a joy.

Penguin Ireland backed me to write this book before I backed myself. Michael McLoughlin sowed the seed early in my mind. He has been relentless along the way in ensuring we write a book that actually makes a difference.

Patricia Deevy provided me with the structure, the system and the discipline needed to write a book. I have been so impressed with her diligence and attention to detail. Patricia, thank you for your support, and for the great drive to make each chapter as good as it can be. Thank you for the many hours of work you have put in.

Of course, I wouldn't have a book to write if I hadn't been blessed in running my business over many years and I have to thank many people who have been instrumental in helping to make McNulty Performance what it is today.

Michael Dempsey has guided me with grace and elegance now for almost ten years. Michael, I never cease to be inspired by your ability to help and to coach.

Stephen Twaddell is a great friend and mentor, as well as a hugely successful businessman. He has always been there for me when I had a tough business decision to make. Stephen has been vital in helping me to create a road map towards our vision.

David Simpson has been a huge influence on me from the very earliest days of my business career. David, thank you for your time and your wisdom. Thank you for caring so much about our team and our clients. Thank you for helping us to navigate the stormy waters along the way.

Michael Kearney is one of the most pragmatic and effective mentors I have ever met. He gives me enough advice in a one-hour meeting to keep me focused in business for six months. Michael, thank you for the support.

Denis O'Brien has given my team and me wonderful business opportunities. He has been a major inspiration through the impact he has made on many thousands of lives through the Digicel Foundation. Denis believed in our business when no one else would. He has been an exceptional entrepreneurial role model for me.

Bernard Murphy – Bernard, your example as a businessman has been a game changer, both for me and for our team. Thank you for your humility, your wisdom and your kindness.

Thank you to all the McNulty Performance team. Thank you for your commitment, drive and dedication. Thank you for keeping our cultural compass front and centre. Thank you for your whatever-it-takes mentality. And thank you for caring about each other and for our clients.

Thank you, too, to all our clients, without whom we wouldn't have a business. Thank you for trusting us, for giving us opportunities to work with and learn from you. Thanks for all the amazing memories and perfect moments along the way. We look forward to many more victories, many more breakthroughs; we look forward to empowering you on the journey towards your potential.

I am very lucky with the people in my life who have inspired me and continue to do so. Words cannot describe how thankful I am to my mum and dad for my wonderful upbringing. You gave my brothers, my sisters and me the freedom, the empowerment and the love to allow us to chase our dreams. Mum and Dad, thank you for creating a fairytale childhood for us and for being amazing every step of the way.

My sisters, Emer and Sarah, have been incredibly supportive and selfless right throughout my life. They have always been encouraging, they have always cheered me along the way. They've helped me in so many ways, from travelling to football games, to running camps and even designing our offices. Their generosity and giving spirit are incredible.

My brothers, Paul, Justin and Patrick, have had a wonderful influence on my life. We used to knock lumps out of each other playing football in the back garden, in games that were as tough and competitive as any. Paul funded me in the first five years in business. Without him, I would have had to pack up and go and get a real job long ago. Justin has been a huge friend and support on the pitch, in the gym and throughout my life. Patrick is the youngest in the family, and the best all-rounder. Thank you, Patrick, for all the love and support along the way.

John Kremer in Queen's University Belfast was the man who first opened up my mind to the possibility of a career in performance psychology. John, thank you for bridging the gap between what you taught in the lecture hall and how that might be applied on the pitch. Thank you for your inspiration and your guidance.

Dessie Ryan, my old friend, coach and mentor. Dessie is one of the most impressive people I have ever met. You have been an inspiration to me, showing how to treat people, how to lead and how to endure in difficult times. Thank you for twenty years of coaching and friendship.

To all my friends and teammates, thank you for the training sessions where you always challenged me to improve. Thank you to all of you for supporting me along the way; on the pitch and off. Thank you for allowing me to disappear from time to time in pursuit of my dreams, and for welcoming me back with undiminished warmth when I returned. Thanks for your positive energy and for your friendship.